POLICE CAMERA ACTION!

POLICE CAMERA ACTION!

Peter Gillbe

Foreword by Alastair Stewart

Ebury Press
London

This book is dedicated to the men and women of our Traffic Police and Air Support Units

First published in 1996

1 3 5 7 9 10 8 6 4 2

Work © Carlton UK Television 1996
Text © Peter Gillbe 1996
Photographs © various (see p.128)

Peter Gillbe has asserted his right to be identified as the author of this work under the Copyright, Designs and Patents Act 1988.

First published in the United Kingdom in 1996 by Ebury Press
Random House, 20 Vauxhall Bridge Road, London SW1V 2SA

Random House Australia (Pty) Limited
20 Alfred Street, Milsons Point, Sydney,
New South Wales 2061, Australia

Random House New Zealand Limited
187 Poland Road, Glenfield, Auckland 10, New Zealand

Random House South Africa (Pty) Limited
PO Box 337, Bergvlei, South Africa

Random House UK Limited Reg. No. 954009

A CIP catalogue record for this book is available from the British Library.

ISBN 0 09 185187 4

Project editor Emma Callery
Designed by Jerry Goldie
Cover designed by Design 23
Original photography by Graham Tann

Printed and bound in Great Britain by Butler and Tanner, Frome, Somerset

Contents

Foreword

The most staggering thing about 'Police, Camera, Action!' is the way it has become an essential part of so many people's viewing. They are clearly getting something special from the programmes which is compelling them to watch, time and again.

For me, one of the most powerful attractions of 'Police, Camera, Action!' is that it highlights the real strengths of our police forces and other emergency services. The police are there to protect us; to prevent crime and accidents, and to help us. Those three objectives are a timeless, unwritten motto which has motivated the police over the years.

In every single programme, we have seen graphic and powerful examples of all three attributes. Sometimes we have seen police stop armed robbers after a high-speed chase through the narrow streets of an otherwise peaceful market town. On another occasion we have seen them use the emergency telephone box to call up and caution an amorous couple who had stopped on the hard shoulder and were engaged in activities that are certainly not in the Highway Code! 'Dull, it isn't', as they say themselves.

Drivers don't always get a ticket, though they often deserve one. Frequently, they just get a ticking off and a useful lesson for future reference. This book contains many of those tips.

'Police, Camera, Action!' also highlights the real skills that police drivers employ to help us. Frequently we have seen them driving at great speed, but with safety to the fore, to catch someone who has done wrong and looks determined to do more: the innocent rarely make a dash for it! But we have also seen them employ the same skills to transport a donor liver across congested London in the rush hour, to get it to a hospital in time for a life-saving operation.

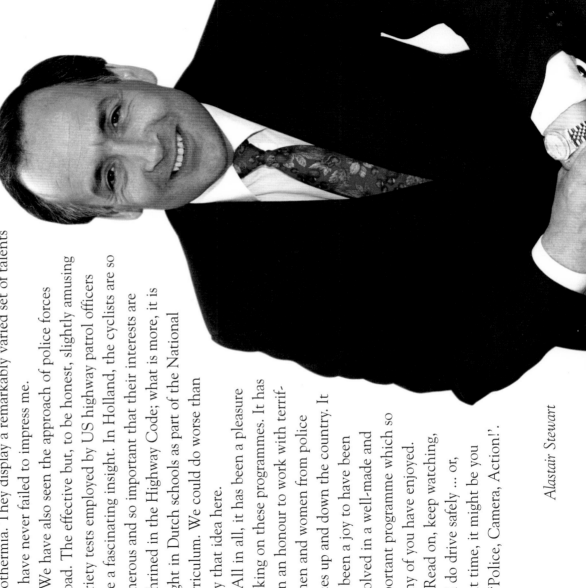

They are good at what they do and they do it for us. Often, they face real horror: the tragedy of death or the ghastliness of multiple injuries. Day in, day out, they carry out tasks we could never do ourselves.

But it is not only at ground level that the police display a potent mixture of skill and compassion: the police helicopter crews (pilots and observers) have become a pivotal part of Britain's emergency services. Again, they deal with crime and human tragedy. They may be helping guide ground forces who are battling with a riotous mob or they may be guiding the same officers to a woman who has fallen while climbing and risks death from hypothermia. They display a remarkably varied set of talents and have never failed to impress me.

We have also seen the approach of police forces abroad. The effective but, to be honest, slightly amusing sobriety tests employed by US highway patrol officers were a fascinating insight. In Holland, the cyclists are so numerous and so important that their interests are enshrined in the Highway Code; what is more, it is taught in Dutch schools as part of the National Curriculum. We could do worse than copy that idea here.

All in all, it has been a pleasure working on these programmes. It has been an honour to work with terrific men and women from police forces up and down the country. It has been a joy to have been involved in a well-made and important programme which so many of you have enjoyed.

Read on, keep watching, and do drive safely ... or, next time, it might be you on 'Police, Camera, Action!'.

Alastair Stewart

Introduction

What is it that makes 'Police, Camera, Action!' the most watched series of factual programmes on British television, with audiences often exceeding 16 million? Programmes about crime and the work of the police often achieve high audience ratings, so what is it that makes this series stand out from the many other excellent productions?

The answer is that it differs from other, apparently similar, programmes in one distinctive way. It is not the police or criminals who are centre stage, but ourselves.

Most of those who we see caught on police video cameras, often breaking the law, or behaving in an irresponsible or thoughtless manner, are not habitual criminals, but people just like us. Whether we admit to it or not, we all have at one time or another been guilty of a misjudgement, a lack of attention, or have broken the rules of the road thinking we could 'get away with it', just that once. Perhaps we have 'got away with it', but in doing so we will have increased the chance of an accident happening and someone getting hurt.

'Police, Camera, Action!' reminds us of just that – what, but for luck, might have happened – and what could happen the next time if we are not so lucky.

The series tries to fulfil that very British description of public service broadcasting by aiming to 'inform, educate and entertain'. It is certainly entertaining, although that is not its primary purpose; it has a strong educational public safety message, but it also

informs us by giving us an insight into the work of the traffic police, how they do their job, and and the technology they use to protect us from ourselves.

After one of the programmes, the British Audience Research Bureau (BARB), carried out some research. It was found that over 60 percent of viewers believed that after they had seen the programme they would be better drivers in the future.

There are few television programmes that actually have any real effect on the way we behave, but if 'Police, Camera, Action!' helps only a small number of us to drive more responsibly, and take more care on the road, it will have done its job.

The First Police

The first uniformed police force in Britain was not set up in London, but in Inverness, where the Inverness Burgh Police were established in 1692. In spite of this, it is Sir Robert Peel who gets the credit for founding the modern police service.

There had been watchmen and beadles in London since the 6th century, but in 1829 Peel established London's Metropolitan Police. Anxious that they should not look like soldiers, their uniform was designed to be civilian, not military. With an eye to practicality, their top hats were built round a framework of strong cane, so that officers could stand on them to look over walls or fences.

Early police regulations meant that all police officers had to wear whiskers, they were required to be on duty for 17 hours out of 24, and had to attend church every Sunday – in uniform of course.

FAST RESPONSE – FROM ROBIN REDBREASTS TO THE FLYING SQUAD

In 1805, a London Horse Patrol was formed to patrol the roads for 20 miles around London to protect travellers from the hundreds of highwaymen who threatened them. Dressed in blue coats, brass buttons, and scarlet waistcoats, they came to be known as the Robin Redbreasts, and were the earliest forerunners of today's fast response units and traffic police patrols.

Following the formation of police forces modelled on the London's Metropolitan police, each major police station had stables for the horses used by mounted officers to patrol their beat, even up to 1920.

The Metropolitan Police Service was quick to see the advantages of the newly invented automobile, and in 1903 bought two 7 hp Wolseley touring cars. However, it was thought they were too good to be used by junior officers to race to the scene of a crime, so they were kept for official use only by the Commissioner and Senior Officers!

It was criminals rather than the police who realised the true potential of the motor car. By 1920, a new type of crime had been invented, the 'smash and grab' raid, and as the police still did not have any operational motor vehicles, criminals were almost guaranteed an easy getaway.

To overcome this, four Crossley vans were used for delivering police stores around London were taken over by a special squad. Equipped with radios and collapsible aerials, they were outstandingly successful against not only the smash and grab raiders, but all kinds of other crimes as well. The unit soon gained the nickname The Flying Squad.

To counter this, criminals in turn obtained faster and more powerful cars. So, in 1927, the Metropolitan Police bought two 1.5 litre Lea-Francis sports cars. With highly tunable engines, they

were capable of speeds in excess of 70 mph. These were the start of a progressively powerful succession of cars, including MG Magnettes, Bentleys, Lagondas, Jaguars and Rovers, that have led to the vehicles that are driven by the police today.

CONTROLS OR TRAPS

The use of video technology to catch motorists speeding is just the latest technique used in the 100-year-old battle to stop motorist's from speeding. Although a law passed in 1865 restricted the new-fangled steam vehicles to walking pace on roads, by insisting that a man with a red flag should walk in front of them, it was in 1896 that the first specific speed limit of 12 miles per hour on all roads became law.

Sometimes it was a single policeman with a stop watch, but anti-speeding techniques gradually became more organised. Officers would measure out a distance, usually of about an eighth of a mile. Then policemen in plain clothes would be positioned at each end of the furlong to time the passing vehicles with stop watches. They would loiter as unobtrusively as

The start of the 'Flying Squad'. Crossley vans equipped with radios and collapsible aerials at Epsom on Derby Day, 1923

Motor Salesman. "THE ENGINE IN THIS CAR, SIR, IS PRACTICALLY IDENTICAL WITH THAT USED BY THE SCOTLAND YARD FLYING SQUAD."
Speed Fiend. "AH, YES—BUT HAVEN'T YOU SOMETHING LIKE THE CAR-BANDITS USE?"

they could until a car came by which was thought to be exceeding the limit. As it passed, the officer started his stop watch and raised a handkerchief to signal his colleague, who would also start his watch. The second timer would raise his handkerchief as the car passed him and both watches would be stopped.

If the car had gone over the speed limit, allowing a small margin for error, they would signal to a 'stopper' – a uniformed police constable hiding further down the road. He would then step out and hold up the car. If both of the stop watches confirmed that the driver had been speeding, he was given a summons. From the start, as now, the police called them speed 'controls' and the public called them speed 'traps'.

Ironically, these first attempts at enforcing speed restrictions were almost universally popular with the public. Car owners were still in a tiny minority and restricted to the well-off, while the press was full of stories about these vehicles which were noisy, smelly, created terrible clouds of dust, and frightened the horses.

Only seven years later things had changed. Most of the objections to automobiles were fading away. There were rapidly increasing numbers on the roads, and they had become generally accepted as a normal part of life. By 1903, when the speed limit was raised to 20 mph, the public was much less sympathetic to the police. Members of the public enjoyed hanging round the speed traps and letting motorists know where the 'trappers' were, while drivers would signal to each other to give similar warning of the speed traps.

The job of the timer was not a popular one with the general public, promoting a feeling of 'them and us' against the police. This enforcement of

One of the first TAGs (Tactical Accident Groups). Consisting of a Wolsely 18/85 saloon and two Triumph T100 solo motorcycles, they were used by London's traffic patrol to deal with serious congestion and accidents.

The Jaguar 3.4 saloon, one of the classic police cars of the 'sixties and 'seventies

the blanket 20 mph speed limit is regarded by police historians as having been the biggest single contribution to the undermining of relations between police and the general public. Even the Automobile Association (AA), which was formed in 1905, was primarily organised to warn motorists of the speed trap. The road patrols, which were initially on push bikes, were not established to assist motorists who had broken down, but had the job of finding where policemen where trying to catch motorists speeding and to warn their members in time.

Everything changed with the 1930 Road Traffic Act. The 20 mph speed limit for private motorists was abolished, and replaced with a 30mph limit in urban areas only, along with a new offence of 'careless driving'. However, proof of this new offence was more difficult for the police to prove and was dependent on circumstances rather than mere timing through a measured distance from a hidden officer. It gave motorists much more scope for an arguable defence.

The very un-English police trap became redundant until the introduction of radar speed traps nearly 30 years later.

Eyespy

It is not just speed that can create danger on the roads, sometimes it is just sheer stupidity or lack of thought! Every day of the year, police and emergency services throughout Britain are involved in the fight against bad driving and car crime. There are now some 24 million vehicles on our roads and whilst most drivers observe the Highway Code, there are many who habitually do not.

Increasingly, the video camera is the most important weapon in the police armoury in capturing those who break the law. Whether it is mounted in a video patrol car, in a helicopter, or at a fixed point along the roadside, the camera images that are collected are more and more important in the fight to make our roads safer.

On watch: driver, observer and video camera

In-car Video

While in the past it was often a case of your word against that of the police, modern police video surveillance techniques provide them with indisputable evidence of the error of your ways. And with the growing number of police video cars on the roads, some marked and many unmarked, there is a growing chance that your bad driving will be recorded on camera.

If your driving offence is considered serious enough to land you in court, then evidence captured on police video equipment may be used against you. The tape recording of the offence is copied, logged, sealed in a tamper-proof evidence bag and then stored in a locked vault until your court appearance. Almost without exception, the tapes in these vaults will convict the driver in question, however much he or she continues to protest their innocence.

Video evidence is so effective that if a motorist who has been stopped claims to be not guilty, all the officers need to do is to play back the tape on the spot and the driver will almost inevitably change his or her mind.

'Police, Camera, Action!' brings you some of that spectacular material. In some cases, it has been used to convict criminals, in others it just shows that, for some drivers, the police are often in the right place at the wrong time.

The majority of in-car video systems used by police forces in the UK are the mobile video/data units called Pro ViDa – short for Proof Video Data. Used for traffic inspection, speed control, and surveillance, they make high quality VHS video recordings of events with the relevant data overlaid on the picture.

ROAD ACCIDENT FACTS

- **96 percent of all transport deaths happen on the roads.**
- **One in seven road deaths is caused by someone who has drunk more than the legal limit.**
- **Just one drink will impair your ability to drive, but if you have twice the legal limit of alcohol in your bloodstream, then you are thirty times more likely to have an accident.**
- **In a 30 mph impact, an adult in a car is thrown forwards with a force of three-and-a-half tons, equal to the weight of an elephant.**
- **The reason that 17-year-olds pay much higher insurance premiums is that they are seven times more likely to have an accident than the average driver.**

The system is made up of five main parts:

- a colour video camera with CCD technology and remote zoom control
- a 'Police Pilot' average speed device with data output and calibration box
- a video data generator box with date/time unit
- a VHS video recorder with remote control unit
- a 4 1/2 inch colour monitor and a 5 3/4 inch LCD colour monitor.

The camera

The CCD 8x zoom camera is usually mounted at the top centre of the windscreen. It has a pan and tilt facility, allowing a target vehicle to be followed, whatever the position of the police vehicle. It has super-fast autofocus with a remote zoom control, a high speed shutter, and controls for white balance and back light.

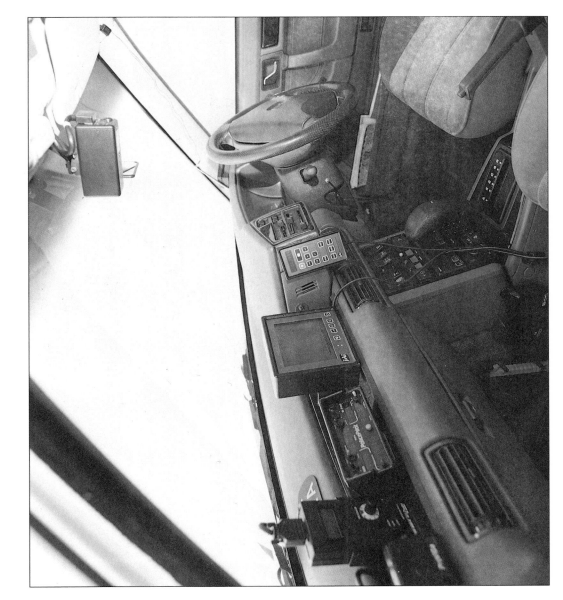

A typical police video car with camera mounted at the top of the windscreen.

The controls for the video equipment are operated by the co-driver.

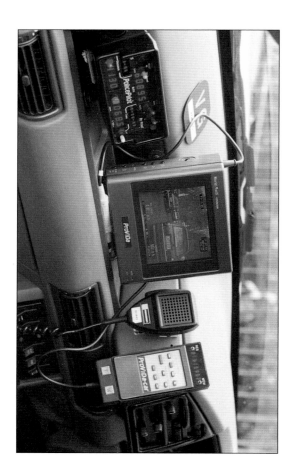

Police pilot

This unit measures the distance and time covered by the patrol car to generate an average speed which is displayed on the monitor and copied by the video cassette recorder. It appears on the bottom left-hand corner of the picture and is labelled PP. The unit has a calibration box usually situated in the glove compartment.

The video data generator

The generator contains the heart of the system and overlays the date, current time, on-going patrol car speed, the Police Pilot average speed with distance and time read out, and a vehicle identification code on to the video picture .

DATE DISPLAY ON MONITOR

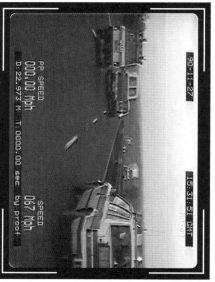

Date	Time
	Vehicle I.D. Code
Police Pilot Average Speed	
Distance	Time	Patrol Car Speed

Access to the video camera is gained by moving the rear seat.

On the latest versions of the system, a frame counter and zoom indicator are included. It also has its own independent power supply to generate data even when the system is turned off or the car battery is disconnected.

The video recorder

The VHS recorder operates off the vehicle's 12-volt power system. Because of the limited space in the passenger compartment, the VCR is often fitted in the boot, but access to it is available by dropping the rear off-side seat. A remote control unit is installed on the front dashboard which has the VCR controls duplicated, together with an LED display showing the a tape counter and time elapsed.

The monitors

There are usually two colour monitors mounted in each vehicle. The 5 ¾ inch LCD colour monitor is generally situated directly in front of the operator, with a 4 ½ inch colour monitor located between the front seats facing backwards towards the rear seats.

Recording the evidence

The success of the system depends not only on its accuracy, but, if required, that its accuracy can be demonstrated in court. So, if you are caught on camera, it is very unlikely you will be able to claim that the equipment was at fault. At the start of every patrol, the Pro ViDa system is checked to ensure it is operating correctly. The system's date and time are checked before inserting a video cassette. The white balance facility on the camera is also adjusted along with back light and high-speed shutter control. A short test recording is then made using all the system's facilities, and this is viewed and checked. The Police Pilot speed detection device is also calibrated and checked. Evidence of these tests being completed is, of course, recorded on the video tape and is also included in any subsequent evidence report.

In Britain, the VCR is recording for the whole of the patrol. In this way, brief or unforeseen incidents are captured on tape when the operator would not otherwise have had time to start the system recording. As sound is being recorded, the operator can give a factual commentary of the incident, including vehicle identification details and a description of the occupants.

Having stopped a suspect vehicle, the driver is given the opportunity to sit in the back of the patrol car and view the tape. Once the motorist sees his or her wrongdoing on camera, it is almost inevitable that they will plead guilty.

If an offence has been committed, and it is possible the tape may be needed as evidence in court, it is taken out of the VCR, the record tag is broken off, an evidence tape label completed and it is bagged and sealed. Back at the police station, a working copy of the tape is made and the master securely locked away.

Road Rage

Road rage has become the popular phrase used to describe aggressive behaviour on the roads. As far as the police are concerned, however, it is not something unique to drivers, but more of an extension of aggressive behaviour by some individuals which could happen in all types of circumstances.

Apart from making driving a stressful and unpleasant experience for everybody on the road, uncontrolled aggression can also be extremely dangerous. Driving on the road is not a race. Reaching your destination safely should be everyone's objective.

When drivers are riled by other road users' deliberate actions, retaliation is just as dangerous and even more childish.

Bumper cars

1. A patrol car came across this lunatic in the middle lane (left of picture). An extremely impatient driver in a pick-up truck was trying to scare a slower driver in front into getting out of the way.

2. But even when that car changed lane to the inside lane to let the pick-up pass, the pick-up driver was so angry that he continued to try and get revenge by driving bumper to bumper. Needless to say, the pick-up driver found himself in court for dangerous driving.

4.

3.

The fool on the hill

3. Only a fool would overtake on a hill ...

4. ... but if this driver continues driving like this, it is only a matter of time before his luck will run out.

6.

5.

Dual

5. In this incident, one white van tried to overtake the other as the road widened to a dual carriageway. However, the overtaking van could not see that roadworks had reduced the dual carriageway to a single lane, and the van in front was determined not to let the other one in.

6. The overtaking van just made it – but look how close it came to hitting the roadworks. Both drivers were stopped by the watching video patrol car.

Boy racers

1. And take the example of this childish battle between a green Escort and white van. As the roadworks caused the two lanes to become one, neither vehicle was willing to give way. Instead of moving into the inside lane at a sensible moment, the van had deliberately left it late so that it could gain a few places in the traffic queue. The green escort, equally stupidly, decided to fight to prevent the van from pushing in.

2. The van managed to push in at the risk of damaging both cars, but by now the driver of the green Escort would not let it rest. Using the temporary extra width provided by the slip road, it decided to cut around the inside to get ahead of the van.

3. Having 'won' the first round, it was the van's turn to try and prevent the Escort cutting in ahead.

4. With the extra width provided by the slip road at an end, both vehicles were trying to fit into space enough for one, and endangering the innocent motorists around them as well. The vehicle behind was sensibly giving these reckless drivers space to play their dangerous game.

5. Eventually the inevitable happened and both vehicles nudged into each other. The van was hanging on the bumper of the car in front of him, but the Escort took advantage and leap-frogged into the space ahead of that car.

6. Unfortunately, for both drivers, they both lost. As the incident had been witnessed and recorded by the police they were both successfully prosecuted.

'POLICE – STOP!'

When a driver is pulled over for speeding by a patrol car it is not radar, but usually VASCAR – The Visual Average Speed Computer and Recorder – or 'Police Pilot', that will have been used to measure the driver's speed. Both work in the same way and they do not have to be linked into a video unit.

A trained officer can use them to check the speed of any vehicle from almost any angle, day or night, in any weather conditions. They work on the same basis as the speed traps of 100 years ago. The basic calculation is that speed equals the distance covered over a measured period of time. The target car is observed moving between any two points and the time this takes is recorded.

The points of measurement commonly used include motorway bridges, painted marks on the road, and junctions. The police car travels along the same distance, recording the time at both the beginning and the end, by pressing a button that feeds the information into a small computer. From the distance and the time to travel it, the machine calculates an average speed and flashes this up on the display unit. On video cars it is included in the on-screen information.

The police car does not have to be following the target car either. It can be ahead of the suspect, when the suspect is first seen crossing a road junction at any angle to the car, when the suspect is approaching from the opposite direction, or when the police car is stationary, having pre-recorded the distance between two reference points on a certain stretch of road.

1.

2.

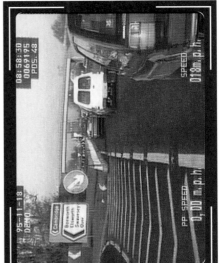

3.

4.

5.

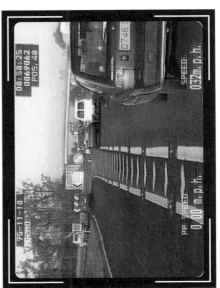

6.

Silly Risks

All of us like to think that we are the safest of drivers – and, of course, most of us are – but quite a few of us occasionally take silly risks in the firm belief that we will get away with it. It is when we take those silly and dangerous risks, however, that we not only imperil our own lives but those of our families and those of complete strangers.

Russian roulette

Level crossings can bring out the worst in some people. It is not only the risk of getting stuck between the two barriers that seems to cause this behaviour, but the real danger of hitting one as it descends – and, unlike in the movies, these steel barriers are not made of soft wood.

1. This driver risked a fine, his licence and his life.

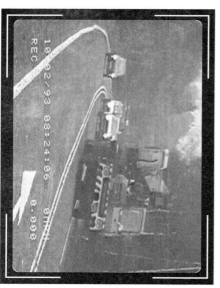

2. The driver of this pick-up was fined as well.

3.

Blind stupidity

3. Fortunately, no one was driving towards this convoy as this driver ignored the double white lines on a blind bend and overtook the long line of vehicles ahead. The results could have been catastrophic. Instead, the driver received a heavy fine and points on his licence.

4.

5.

6.

7.

Too close

4+5. Aggressive overtaking is not only illegal but life threatening – particularly when it takes place on blind bends as it did in this case.

Tailgating

Following too closely to the vehicle in front, or tailgating, is dangerous. It may frustrating to be held up when you are in a hurry, but trying to force another driver to speed up or get out of the way is downright dangerous.

6. This lorry driver had not spotted that he was tailgating an unmarked police video car.

7. And neither had this driver – he was obvious-ly desperate to get past. If the police car had been forced to stop, the driver of the white car would have had virtually no chance of avoiding an accident. He might as well have been on an ice rink for all the chance he had of avoiding a collision.

Speed Control

If you lose control of your car, the consequences are serious, not only for you, but also for those around you using the roads. The ability to stop safely can be a matter of life and death, and staying alive can be as easy as giving yourself plenty of time and space. But bad driving conditions are not the only reason we should drive with extra care. Losing concentration at the wheel, whatever the circumstances, can be just as hazardous.

Too fast ...

1. The driver of the blue Rover approached these traffic lights far too fast ...

2. ... and lost control of his car as he skidded to a halt in a cloud of blue smoke.

... and too late

3+4. Cones, road signs and markings are there for a purpose, and are meant to be heeded, but this speeding motorist barely slowed down as he approached a built-up area, and he completely ignored the 40 mph limit. He was totally unprepared when a dog crossed the road in front of him. It was lucky there were no pedestrians on the pavement.

1. 6:46:48 80

2. 6:46:50 68

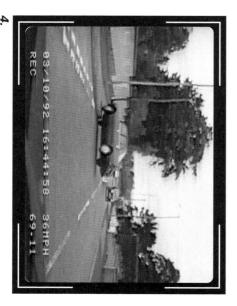

3. 03/10/92 16:44:53 75MPH 1-029

4. 03/10/92 16:44:58 36MPH REC 69-11

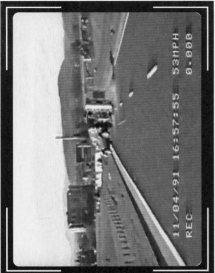

5.

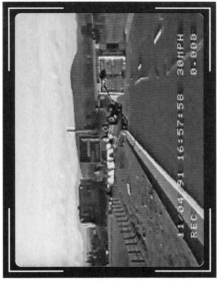

6.

7.

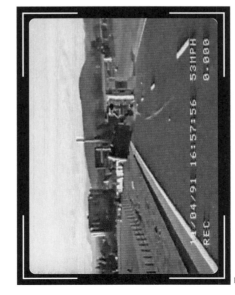

8.

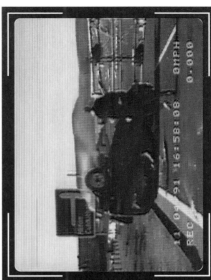

9.

Blown away

5 – 9. Even for the most careful drivers, there are unexpected hazards. This caravan was caught by a sudden gust of wind near Inverness. Police advise caravan drivers to stay off the roads in blustery conditions but their advice is not always taken. Luckily, when the officer went to help the occupants of the car, he found them shaken but not seriously injured.

Dangerous Loads

Unsafe loads are accidents waiting to happen. Unfortunately, there is no shortage of drivers not thinking of the implications of their carelessness, whether it is a do-it-yourself enthusiast hoping that he can get away with transporting an outsize piece of wood back home on a family saloon car not designed to take large loads, or an HGV driver not bothering to check the dimensions or the security of the load.

1.

2.

Irish jig

1+2. The Irish may be renowned for their dancing, but who would have imagined the local plant machinery in Belfast also knew a jig or two.

Twister

3. This mobile home was on the move in more ways than one. It could have twisted all the way round to block the carriageway or even fallen off the back of the lorry.

Pile up

4. Having a car hit you is one thing, but one falling on you from above is quite another! One thin strap was all that was holding these three car wrecks in place, and one sharp bend could have been enough to cause yet more wrecks on the highway.

3.

4.

Thick as a plank

5. The video patrol car crew could hardly believe their eyes when they saw this motorcyclist (below) in Liverpool. History does not record whether, having stopped the bike, the officers made any comparisons with the thickness of the plank.

5.

6.

Two inches too big

6. Some loads are not dangerous in themselves, it is just when the drivers fail to check the height of their loads. Another inch or two and this lorry (above) would have brought down the whole bridge rather than just a shower of concrete debris.

Scrap on wheels

7+8. This mini attracted the attention of police in Poole because they were concerned by its poor condition. Between the excessive rust, the wings flapping in the wind, the holes in the chassis and the defective lights, it was more a question of what was right with it rather than what was wrong with it.

The Dorset Police weren't surprised to learn that the owners of the car had paid just £5 for it. What did surprise them, however, was that they had manage to drive it 75 miles from Bristol!

There was no way the police were going to let them drive it back again. The students did not get charged, but the car had to be scrapped there and then. But our impoverished scholars left happy – they got £10 more from the scrap yard than the £5 they paid for it.

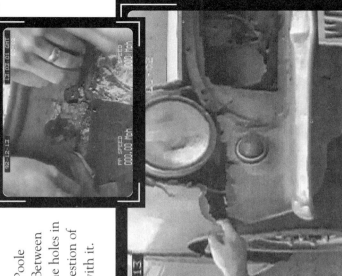

7.

8.

Sheer Stupidity

It is not just speed that can create danger on the roads, sometimes it is just sheer stupidity or lack of thought! Many of us push our luck on occasions, such as going a little too fast, leaving it a little late as the traffic lights turn red, using a mobile phone while driving, parking on double yellow lines, or any one of a hundred other things. On each occasion we may not cause an accident, or get caught in the act – but each time there is a greater chance of something going wrong.

Not so good to talk

1. The driver of this four-wheel drive vehicle was spotted by police using his mobile phone while driving, and although he managed to negotiate a round-about with reasonable success, eventually the road made him pay the price for not paying attention.

2. With his mind far from the road, the driver failed to spot the potential danger of a car pulling up at a crossing ahead. He may have escaped a crash, but not the police. He was penalised for driving without due care and attention.

Shut it!

3. It may be obvious that the first thing you do after getting into your car is to shut the door, but this driver could not even manage that properly – as he discovered the first time he went round a corner!

1.

2.

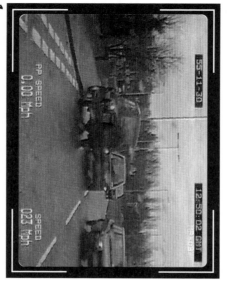

3.

4.

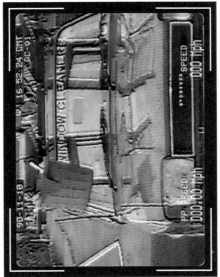

5.

7.

The slow lane?

4. When the South Yorkshire police first noticed this car (right of picture), it was travelling in the middle lane of the motorway at 65 mph. There was an animated telephone conversation going on and the driver was paying scant attention to the road. It was little wonder then that he failed to notice his speed drop to 45 mph which was causing traffic to stack up behind him.

One rung short of a ladder?

5. With sponges, chamois leather and ladders hanging over the car, it did not take an aspiring Sherlock Holmes long to deduce the profession of these intrepid entrepreneurs driving their red Capri. What was more difficult to fathom is why a bucket had been so strategically placed as to obscure the driver's vision.

The expensive short cut

Pavements are intended to provide a safe area for the person travelling on foot, and it seems a particularly aggressive violation when hijacked by four wheels. There is certainly no disguising this blatant and potentially dangerous short cut.

6. Unable to wait for a few more seconds while the lights changed, the Metro not only went up onto the pavement to cut the corner ...

7. ... but through the building as well! However, he did not feel so clever when he was pulled over and told his performance had been recorded. It not only cost him the time he thought he had saved, but a fine and penalty points, too.

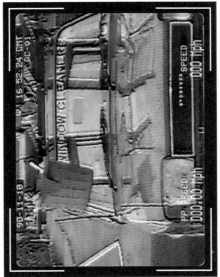

6.

There's none so blind...

1. What this van driver could clearly see is a cyclist just in front of him. But so eager was he to get to his destination that he simply pretended the cyclist was not there and cut across in front of her.

...as those who will not see

2. Other drivers stopped at the zebra crossing to let the women cross, but not so the driver of the Golf on the left.

3. Now followed by a police video car, he just missed an old lady at the next crossing only 100 metres/yards up the road. In the space of a minute, he had committed the same offence twice. Is your time more valuable than someone else's life? This driver obviously thought his was.

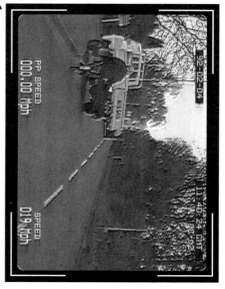

The new bus lane!

4. It is not only private cars that break the law. Pavements should be the sole preserve of the pedestrian, but this bus driver in a hurry had other ideas.

Booked

5. And if you need a road atlas, buy one at a shop. These two motorists (left of picture) were caught passing a book of maps from one car to the other. They both got booked.

5.

Order booked

6. In their rear view mirror, West Mercia Police noticed a van being driven erratically and turned their camera around to record it on video. The driver was certainly unaware of the camera, and with his attention diverted as he wrote up orders in his order book, he was largely unaware of the road ahead. It was clearly dangerous and an offence the police take extremely seriously. It cost this driver a £120 fine and six points on his licence

6.

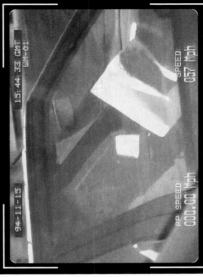

7.

Map reader

7. Don't try to sort out your route en route, like this driver did, as it will lead you into the arms of the law.

Videobikes

It is not only police cars and helicopters that are equipped with video cameras. In some parts of the country there are solo video motorcycles as well. The camera is so small that in its usual position under the headlights, it is hardly noticeable. And with no television screen in sight, as it would be a distraction to the rider, it is virtually impossible for the casual observer to tell if a police motorcycle is equipped with video or not. The cassette recorder is mounted in the panniers, as is an LCD monitor which can be brought out to replay tapes of an offence and show the guilty motorist the error of his ways.

Over the limit

1. A police video motorcycle came across this driver who appeared to think the road was dual not single carriageway. She was swerving so far over to the right on the bends that she was going on to the verge!

2. The driver was three-and-a-half times over the limit and was extremely lucky not to injure herself or anyone else. She was banned from driving for 18 months and was fined more than £500. Just one drink will impair your ability to drive, but if you have twice the legal limit of alcohol in your bloodstream, then you are thirty times more likely to have an accident. The truth of the matter is that drinking means you can't assess speed and distances accurately and you really do delude yourself that you are the safest person on the road.

1.

2.

You've Been Gatsoed

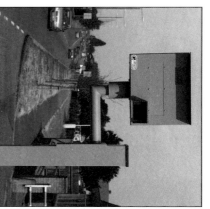

The next time you slow down when you catch sight of one of those grey boxes containing a speed camera by the side of the road, or worse still, you notice a flash from the camera in your rear view mirror, remember one man, Maurice Gatsonides, or Gatso to his friends. And you should thank him because has been responsible for the thirty years of technology that has undoubtedly saved many thousands of lives.

For sixty years, motorists were caught speeding by the same method used since the turn of the century, being timed with stopwatches through a measured distance. Gatso was, and at 85 still is, a Dutch car enthusiast and rally driver. He did not object to motorists, sometimes including himself, being caught speeding, but he objected to unfair prosecutions based on what he considered to be a totally inaccurate timing system.

Once when accused of speeding when he knew he had slowed down, he checked the distance which the police said was 100 metres, and found it was only 87 metres! And with his rally experience he knew the limitations of pre-quartz stopwatches.

He decided to find a better way. He devised an electrical timing system that would be accurate to the hundredth of a second. Then the measured distance need only be 10 metres. To eliminate human error, it was activated by a vehicle tyre running over rubber tubes stretched across the road.

These units were successful, in spite of some motorists discovering that if they locked their wheels over the rubber tube it was likely to destroy the tube! The next stage was for Gatso to replace the rubber tube with a radar speed measurement system, and combine this with a hi-speed camera. So today we have the grey GATSO boxes on roadside posts which are a familiar sight in countries throughout the world.

Alongside these speed cameras, GATSO also developed another variation, the 'red light camera'. This is able to take two pictures in sequence of vehicles crossing junctions when the traffic lights are red.

More than half the police forces in Britain now have traffic enforcement cameras, with the greatest number of permanent Gatso sites in the London area. The fact that they are as much a

Maurice Gatsonides (below), Monte Carlo Ralley winner, displays the Barclays Bank Challenge Cup.

One of the growing number of roadside 'flashers'.

When one of the first Gatso cameras was installed at traffic lights in Jackson Missouri, its two pictures taken one second apart captured the result of a car jumping a red light.

successful deterrent against speeding as they are providers of prosecution evidence, is acknowledged by the fact that most units are only equipped with a camera at random times, although many may still have a detector and a flash unit.

While a guilty driver may notice the flash of the cameras in his mirrors, in most cases it is only when an optional fixed penalty notice for £40 and three licence endorsement points arrives on your door step, that you know you have been Gatsoed. Perhaps disappointingly, the pair of incriminating pictures are not sent, but only made available if you plead not guilty. Very few of those pleas succeed.

In spite of advertisements in the motor press for special trick number plates that are supposedly unphotographable, there is no legal way of beating the GATSO, and it is illegal to drive a car with its registration number obscured.

In Britain, unlike some other countries, GATSO cameras photograph from behind, so the drivers cannot be positively identified. If a notice of prosecution is issued, the car's owner must state who was driving at the time otherwise the owner is liable. It is illegal to nominate someone else, even if they are prepared to have your penalty points on their licence.

If you want to know where GATSO cameras are sited, the Clever Map company publishes the London Speed Trap Map, which is now in its seventh edition and has sold 60,000 copies. But beware! There is no distinction made between which units have cameras and which are just flashing dummies, and Gatso units are constantly being installed in new locations – and they are coming in different guises. Mobile speed cameras are being used to check speeds through motorway roadworks where there is a temporary speed limit. Portable units are also being used to catch drivers speeding on roads which may not need permanent units.

It is the fact that the cameras exist at all that saves lives. All the research shows that the mere presence of the units, and the possibility that you may be caught on camera, succeeds in slowing traffic to the legal limit. Both the numbers of accidents and deaths are substantially reduced.

Nearly a third of all accidents are caused by excessive speed, and it is still one of the most common ways of breaking the law on Britain's roads and motorways. With the reduction of vehicle speed a road safety priority, there are going to be a lot more grey boxes by the side of roads. And hopefully we will be driving slowly enough to notice them.

Motorway Cameras

The police have a number of fixed cameras at strategic positions along our motorways which feed their pictures back to control rooms. Although the images are continually monitored, there has often been only one video recorder switched between sixty or more cameras, so a sudden event is less likely to be caught on tape than an incident that develops more slowly. However, this is rapidly changing as the latest developments in cost-effective video technology allow multiple cameras to be recorded simultaneously.

It is to the control rooms that the roadside phones are connected. When you use one, its location is automatically displayed and the police will know exactly where you are the moment you lift up the receiver. There are specially trained operators who can cope with any emergency, and notify a breakdown truck or send for the emergency services.

With your location identified, the control room can often use one of the cameras to focus in on you to make sure you are safe. Unfortunately, but perhaps inevitably, there is a growing habit of drivers using their mobile phone to call in for help instead. They may save you a short walk to a roadside phone, but most drivers do not know exactly where they are, or often even which motorway they are on, and this can cause major delays in locating the vehicle in need.

Motorway Control

At the Central Motorway Police Group control room at Perry Barr, a combined operation between the West Midlands and West Mercia police forces, they monitor 64 cameras covering 74 miles of motorway. From the motorway control rooms, officers can spot breakdowns, any accidents, and often record incidents that range from the criminally stupid, to the simply bizarre.

Very Mobile Homes

Some incidents happen when you least expect them. An officer on a hoist was installing a new camera on the M27 in Hampshire when he got the shock of his life.

1. A lorry with trailer (top right of picture)was carrying mobile homes on the inside lane, when its driver was alarmed by another lorry joining from the slip road. The lorry and trailer swerved only very slightly to avoid the other vehicle approaching from its left, but this was enough to break the coupling to the trailer, which then rolled free.

2. The trailer and its load crossed the outside lane ...

3. bounced across the central reservation ...

4. crossed both lanes of on-coming traffic

5. ... and overturned on the verge.

This could have been a catastrophe. But thanks to some amazing luck and the fast reactions of some drivers, there was no damage to any other car. The moral of this incident is always to expect the unexpected on the roads.

1.

2.

3.

4.

5.

Fire!

A car in flames is mercifully something you see more often in the movies than in real life. Nevertheless, our vehicles do contain large quantities of highly flammable materials, and while an exploding petrol tank may be rare, fires do happen, and often for very mundane reasons. A leaking fuel cap, an electrical fault or a cigarette not properly extinguished, can often lead to a highly dangerous situation.

This camper van had just caught fire. Its two occupants had managed to salvage a few bits from it, but all they could then do was to watch forlornly from a distance until help arrived. If your car ever catches fire when you are driving, the safest thing to do is to stop, get out of the car as soon as possible and call the fire brigade. Trying to deal with the situation yourself often makes things worse. Opening the bonnet fans the flames, as the fire will only get bigger when it has access to more oxygen, and most car-sized fire extinguishers are sorely inadequate for the job they are designed for, so don't bank on them. We would also do well to follow the example of these van owners who took the wise precaution of standing well away from the blaze which very quickly spread throughout the entire vehicle.

1. In the space of three minutes, the van turned from a cloud of smoke into an inferno. The fire brigade were on the scene within 15 minutes but it was too late to save this van which was completely gutted. But the danger is never past until the fire is out.

1.

2.

3.

IF YOUR CAR CATCHES FIRE

Don't panic. Stop the car quickly and safely. Get everyone out of the car and make sure they move at least 12 metres/40 feet away. Don't open the bonnet and don't try to extinguish the fire yourself.

4.

2. Sometimes even the professionals are taken by surprise. An exploding petrol tank such as this can easily throw dangerous metal debris across the width of a motorway carriageway.

3. It is not just the petrol tank that can go up. The heat caused the spare tyre on the front of the van to explode. In a severe blaze it could have been the road tyres as well. With clouds of smoke threatening the safety of other drivers, the police took the extra precaution of closing the three lanes of the motorway until the danger had passed.

4. The prompt and intelligent reaction of the occupants saved their lives, but their prized possession was reduced to a burnt-out shell.

Distractions

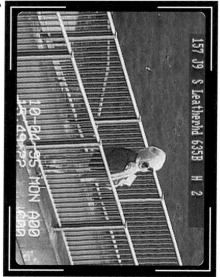

When driving, on motorways in particular, it is easy to let our concentration wander, and we can forget about the potential dangers that exist on the roads all of the time. Many serious accidents are caused by just that lack of concentration when we allow ourselves to be distracted by incidents taking place along the roadside. However, sometimes it is quite difficult not to take a second look at some things you see on the roadside.

Mr Blobby

1. Mr Blobby is distracting at the best of times and especially when he appears unexpectedly. A student had apparently been raising funds for a College charity rag week and was on his way home when he decided to give an impromptu performance to motorists on the M25.

2. The police Range Rover stopped below, not for an autograph, but to direct the traffic out of the overtaking lane because of an accident 200 metres/yards ahead. In a situation like this, the last thing drivers need is another distraction.

Balloon

3. There are more attractive sights than Mr Blobby but it was a miracle that an accident didn't happen on this occasion with everyone rubber-necking a hot air balloon.

LASER SPEED GUN

The most common cause of road traffic accidents is inappropriate or excessive speed. It is estimated that in Britain, 1200 deaths a year are due to speeding. In fact, last year alone, half a million motorists paid £30 million in speeding fines.

Many of them will have been captured on hand-held Radar Speeding Detectors, technology which has been in use since 1959. Its disadvantages are that heavy traffic can restrict how effective it is, and that motorists need to be stopped so that they can be booked.

For the last five years an increasing number of GATSO fixed speed cameras have stood sentry at the side of our roads, successfully slowing traffic streams and providing photographic evidence of speeding drivers. But they have problems too. Drivers learn where they are, slow down to pass and then speed up as soon as they are out of range, and a succession of offending motorists can quickly use up the limited amount of film carried by the camera.

But things are about to change as the latest technology, in the shape of the new Laser Speed Gun, becomes operational. Using a reflected low-power laser beam instead of radar, they are more accurate and can be used over greater distances. The new speed guns have all the advantages of both Radar Guns and GATSO cameras – and with none of their disadvantages. Hidden at the roadside, these hand-held devices will not only photograph the speeding drivers, but also print up the time, date, reference number and speed of any number of successive offenders. All the evidence required for conviction is supplied ready for the notice of prosecution to be sent to the guilty driver.

The laser speed guns can be hand held or mounted on a tripod.

Crash

Hazardous weather conditions can make driving especially difficult, particularly when cars don't maintain their distance from one another. On 6 August 1991, cameras on the M6 caught one of the worst pile-ups ever recorded.

1. Heavy summer traffic in the hot dry weather had polished the road surface. The police and emergency services knew that all it needed was for rain to make the roads slippery and there would be the inevitable accidents.

2. The weather changed rapidly and there was a sudden downpour. Most drivers slowed down because of the rain and heavy surface water, but traffic quickly began to speed up again when the sun returned. However, many drivers didn't realise just how slippery the roads had become, and continued to travel too fast and too close to each other. It was only a matter of time until ...

3. It all started with a red Vauxhall Cavalier speeding in the outside lane.

4. The driver failed to anticipate the vehicles in front slowing down and had to take evasive action.

5. It swerved into the centre lane, but the driver lost control.

6. In his attempt to straighten out he hit the central barrier.

7. As it left the picture, the red Cavalier hit the white lorry in the inside lane, but the driver did not stop and the car has never been traced.

8. Some cars were forced to slow down or stop, while others, like the red lorry, took evasive action by pulling onto the hard shoulder.

1.

2.

3.

4.

5.

6.

7.

8.

9.

10.

11.

12.

13.

14.

ACCIDENT STATISTICS FOR 1995

10 people a day are killed on Britain's roads and 850 are injured.

In 1995 there were a total of 3,621 deaths:

1,038	pedestrians
213	cyclists
445	motorcyclists
1,749	car users
35	in buses and coaches
126	in goods vehicles
15	other

In 1995 there were a total of 310,506 road users injured:

47,029	pedestrians
24,913	cyclists
23,480	motorcyclists
193,992	car users
9,269	in buses and coaches
10,526	in goods vehicles
1,297	other

9. But some drivers were still travelling too fast and could not react in time, such as the white lorry in the middle lane. The driver skidded into the car in front and ended up blocking the inside lane as well.

10. Simultaneously, a car driver in the overtaking lane hit the car in front and a succession of speeding cars started a multiple pile-up.

11 – 13. In less than a minute, one side of the M6 was completely blocked, including the hard shoulder.

14. Although some of the vehicles immediately behind managed to slow down in time, the cars and lorries who were following them did not.

15. An articulated lorry then jackknifed into the central reservation and blocked all three lanes as more and more vehicles ploughed into it. Six people, some of whom were injured, were prosecuted for driving without due care and attention, although luckily no one was killed. In circumstances such as these, the best thing to do is to pull right off the carriageway, leaving the hard shoulder free for the emergency services to get through – something they were unable to do on this occasion.

15.

Helicops

From the time a request for assistance has been received, a helicopter crew can be airborne in a matter of minutes, and with flying speeds of up to 140 miles an hour, their rapid response times can prove invaluable.

The Aerospatiale AS 355N Twin Squirrel, registered as G–DPPS, used by Dyfed Powys police is typical of the helicopters in use by police Air Support Units in the UK and is both fast and economical.

It is equipped with a Leo 400TV/SPIR optical system on the front of the helicopter. This gyroscopically stabilized pod contains a colour camera with a 15 x zoom capability that can be used either for panoramic surveillance or zoomed in close for person and vehicle licence plate recognition. The helicopter also has an 8 x zoom thermal imaging camera with image freezing for detail investigation, image enhancement and user set temperature alarm levels for search and rescue detection.

At the rear of the Twin Squirrel is a Nite-Sun, 30 million candle-power searchlight, which at a height of 300 metres will illuminate an area the size of a football pitch, or the beam can focus down to the size of the penalty area.

In the centre of the fuselage there are the four speakers of a Skyshout, 400-watt public address system which can easily be heard on the ground above the noise of the helicopter when it is at 150 metres. This also incorporates a siren.

To top it off, the Twin Squirrel also carries Fujinon Stabiscope 14x zoom stabilized binoculars, additional still and video cameras, and stretcher and survival equipment for use in search and rescue operations. Quite a machine.

Air History

There are now 21 Police Air Support Units spread throughout Britain, but it has taken over three quarters of a century for the technology to catch up with police requirements.

The first step was taken on Derby Day in 1920, when a police observer was taken up in an aircraft loaned from the RAF to report on traffic conges-

tion on the approaches to Epsom racecourse. The first lesson learnt was that because the plane did not have a wireless the only way it could pass on information was by landing again.

Next year's Derby Day saw several innovations; an airship rather than an aircraft was used, allowing the observer to remain in the best position for viewing the traffic, and a radio transmitter allowed messages to be sent by morse code to the police control room in the main grandstand. At the same time, an RAF aircraft took photographs of the congestion so that the police could analyse the traffic conditions at their leisure.

Over the following years, more trials continued using both fixed wing airplanes, which were too fast and airships, which were at the mercy of the weather. And both were too expensive for anything other than use on special occasions. Police forces knew what they needed, but the problem was that the technology designed to satisfy that need did not yet exist.

Although helicopters were not to be developed for another ten years, the 1932 Derby Day saw the first police use of an autogiro. Autogiros use unpowered helicopter-type rotors to give lift, but they require a conventional propeller to give forward speed and to get the horizontal propeller to turn. Their advantages are that they are very cheap to run and, although they cannot hover like a helicopter, they can fly at speeds as low as 25 mph, ideal for observing what is going on below.

It was not the Metropolitan Police that found an answer to the high costs of flying, but the Reigate Borough Police. In 1936, they persuaded pilots at the local flying club to volunteer as Special Constables and, with the pilots' own aircrafts, the first Police Air Section was created. Composed of seven light fixed-wing aircrafts and an autogiro, the section operated successfully until the start of the Second World War.

This 1914 cartoon (above) anticipated the use of police airships by seven years!

The R33 airship (below) flew nearly 600 miles in police service on Derby Day in 1921.

A police Cierva C30P autogiro at the 1935 Wembley Cup Final.

Autogiros and light planes may have done the job adequately, but it was another 18 years before the real solution, helicopters, developed during the Second World War, began to be used by the police. Post-war austerity meant that there was no money for luxuries such as police aircraft, and in 1950 the Home Office took the view that helicopters would not ever be of much use to the police. However the police forces knew otherwise, and by 1953 trials had started.

It was not just aviation technology that was leaping ahead. The first demonstration of 'heli-tele', the use of an aerial television camera was in 1956. Although the pictures were of poor quality by today's standards, and range was limited, pictures could be sent directly to the ground.

Helicopters were expensive to operate, and some police forces continued to use cheaper, conventional aircraft. But by 1980, with the availability of powerful Night-Sun floodlights, Skyshout public address equipment, more sophisticated television cameras, both standard and infrared, and more reliable helicopters, the police had the technology they needed. The day of the Air Support Units had arrived, and they have now become an essential part of Britain's police service.

Blue Astra

Not surprisingly, some of the most aggressive driving witnessed by the police is committed by criminals trying to avoid arrest. Drivers are rarely aware of the fact that there may be a helicopter tracking them, but once it is called in, there is no escape. This example is typical.

1. The Dyfed Powys Police Air Support Unit were monitoring the police radio and heard that a blue Astra had made off from a garage without paying for petrol. The Unit scrambled and quickly located the car, which turned out to be stolen. From the air they were able to advise South Wales Police ground forces.

2. In this case, desperate to escape, the criminals recklessly drove the car up the outside of a long traffic queue, knocking into many of the stationary vehicles.

3. The ground forces attempted to block off the Astra's escape route but the police car positioned across the carriageway was rammed.

One passenger was immediately seized while the other two men tried to get away, but were caught a short distance away.

All three offenders were jailed and banned from driving for three years. The driver, who was found to be driving under the influence of drugs, had his prison sentence doubled both for his driving offences and for causing actual bodily harm to the sergeant in the rammed police car.

1.

2.

3.

No Hiding Place

In this instance, all the helicopter crew had to do was to direct the ground forces towards a stolen red digger, fitted with Tracker (see page 57), which was located in a farmyard. It could be identified easily from the air even though it was well hidden behind the yellow lorry.

1.

2.

1+2. Helicopter observer: *Keep coming, keep coming, go beyond the Volkswagen on your right, keep going beyond the concrete wall on your left. There is a gap, go through the gap.*

Go right, go right, there is a yellow lorry with a crane on the back. At the back of that is the plant, the digger in question. Over. Patrol Vehicle: *990 Foxtrot. Yes we have located the digger. We've got the owner of the yard here. He has stated that he let a corner of the yard to two Irish males.*

We've got two items of plant machinery equipment here and a trailer as well so we'll have to start treating them as suspicious.

Not only did the owner of the yard not know the stolen vehicle was there, he also didn't know about the additional £250,000 worth of stolen plant machinery the police subsequently found.

HELICOP – FACTS

- In 1995, the South East Region Air Support Unit, the busiest in the country, responded to a total of 5,300 calls and assisted in 626 arrests.
- The average helicopter patrol time is one-and-a-half hours, but can be up to three-and-a-quarter hours.
- Helicopter cameras were first used operationally at the 1977 Notting Hill Carnival.
- Helicopter cameras can identify licence plates at up to 300 metres.

The Silver Saab

At the scene of an armed robbery in Oxford, a member of the public reported seeing the gang using a silver Saab as their getaway car. This was the only clue Thames Valley Police had to work on. The helicopter called in to search the area soon spotted the car travelling recklessly along the road at more than 90 mph. The helicopter radioed ground forces and alerted them to the position of the bandit vehicle.

1. The criminals, realising the police were in pursuit, were determined to get rid of anything incriminating, but the video camera clearly recorded a gun being thrown out of the car. This visual evidence later proved useful in court.

5.

6.

2. Despite the road coming to an end, the robbers pressed on, across a field. But there was no way out. Forced to abandon their car, the two men continued on foot.

3. As they found their way out onto the road, they must have felt their luck was in. A potential getaway vehicle, a white van, was just leaving the close.

4. A struggle ensued but the driver was no pushover. He was determined that his van was not going to provide the criminals with an escape route and he walked away with the keys. It might have been a different story if they had still been armed.

5. The criminals continued running, but with the police closing in they had no option but to give themselves up.

6. The helicopter's valuable evidence helped secure a conviction – they each got nine years.

TRACKER AND TRAK-BAK

Britain has a higher rate of car theft than any country in the EC. Although car crime in general is falling, an increasing number of vehicles disappear for ever and police helicopters are playing an important new role in the fight against car theft.

The latest tracking technology means that the police can find over 95 percent of stolen vehicles fitted with the commercially available Tracker and TrakBak devices. These are based on radio transmitters hidden in your car that work like a homing device. The units can be placed in your vehicle in more than thirty places so the thief has very little chance of finding it, even you won't know where it is.

TrakBak is activated as soon as the car is broken in to and will display its location on a map in a control room. The police are then guided to the vehicle.

Tracker is activated as soon as you tell the police you car has been stolen. Tracker sends out a homing signal. Helicopters and cars are fitted with receivers that pick up the signals and allow the stolen car to be traced.

Thermal Imaging

Thermal imaging, one of the latest developments in traffic surveillance technology, gives new meaning to the expression 'in hot pursuit'. Police helicopters are now equipped with thermal imaging cameras which are heat, rather than light, sensitive.

The thermal imaging camera responds to the body's temperature so day or night, the police can follow their target wherever it goes. And from the ground, there is no way of knowing when this camera is being used so, as our this fugitive discovered, if the police are tracking someone, they can run but they can't hide.

Mountain rescue

On a wet, cold September morning, the Dyfed Powys police were called to help in the search for a woman who had gone missing on a mountain walk.

1. Carrying out a systematic search of a large area of open ground and forestry, they soon found a heat source at the edge of the forest where the woman had slipped and fallen.

2. She had hurt her ankle and was desperately cold – much longer and hypothermia would have set in. To have accurately searched the same area on foot would have taken 20 police officers at least a week – almost certainly too long.

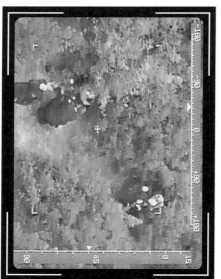

1.

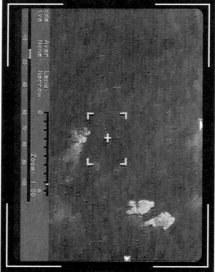

2.

THERMAL IMAGING TECHNOLOGY

The thermal imager works by detecting and measuring the differences in the radiated temperature of any object or surface. This means that the operator can, in effect, see in the dark and through clouds or undergrowth.

The first thermograms, or heat pictures, were made as early as 1840 by Sir William Herschel and his son John. But it has taken 150 years for a lightweight, sophisticated system to be developed. Even as recently as 1960, it took 10 minutes for commercial thermal imaging systems to produce a single thermal picture, and required a mains power supply and heavy equipment. Today the latest systems weigh only 7 kg and are about the size of a shoe box.

For police use they are mounted in a gyroscopically stabilised, fully directional camera pod mounted on the front of the aircraft. This pod contains a 15 x zoom colour TV camera as well as a zoom forward-looking, infrared (FLIR) thermal imager. The pod can pan infinitely through 360 degrees or tilt up and down to cover a wide angle.

The pod is controlled by the police observer with a laptop control unit, and he is able to view the pictures on a TV monitor mounted in front of him. As well as being able to record incidents on the on-board video cassette recorder, microwave down links can be used to transmit live thermal images or TV pictures to either a central or mobile command centre for operation control. Data such as time, date, frame count and zoom factor can be superimposed on the screen, and also geographical positioning system (GPS) information from satellites, confirming the second by second position of the aircraft for evidential purposes.

Hot pursuit

1. The driver of this stolen car did not realise that as he drove faster, the car became hotter – which made it easier and easier for the police helicopter to track.

2. The engine glowed white – shining like a beacon for its pursuer, and, like an airplane laying down a vapour trail, the car exhaust was clearly visible.

3. When he tried to make a run for it, the fugitive was even more obvious to the police in the helicopter above.

4. Even when he tried to hide from the helicopter behind a bush, his body heat gave him away.

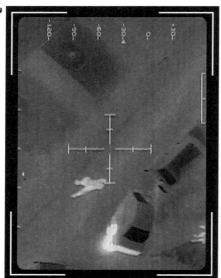

3.

1.

4.

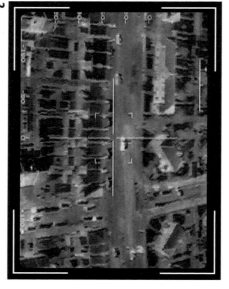

2.

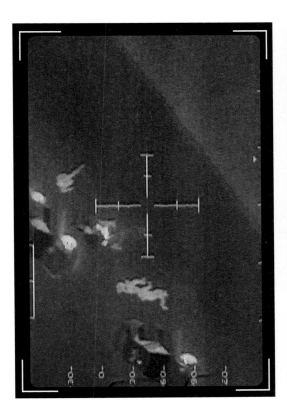

5. It was only a matter of time before the ground forces were guided to the spot by the aerial observer and the fugitive was arrested.

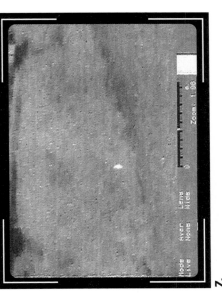

6.

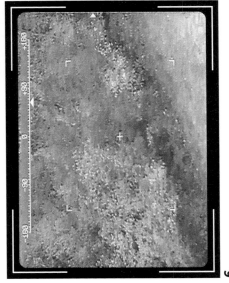

7.

8.

Daylight robbery

These images from the Dyfed Powys Air Support Unit show just how effective the thermal imager can be during daylight hours. A car thief had abandoned a stolen vehicle and run off to hide in the undergrowth, but his attempt to conceal himself was hopeless.

6. In daylight he is well hidden from view from pursuing officers on the ground – even at close range.

7. But on the thermal imaging camera, a white heat source is visible.

8. Sure that this heat source was the criminal they were after, the helicopter directed two CID officers to the exact location, and they quickly arrested the suspect.

Blind man's buff

At night what can be hidden to the naked eye is obvious to the thermal imaging camera on the helicopter and the helicopter observer can talk by radio directly to officers on the ground. Following a call from a member of the public about a man behaving suspiciously, local police officers who arrived were unable to find him in the dark. However, the helicopter was quickly on the scene and spotted a suspect in a garden. By talking to the officers on the ground directly, they were able to guide them to the man hiding behind some bushes.

1. Observer to ground: *The officer standing by a fence, by a garage wall, right outside by an area car. If you could just listen to my instructions please.*

If you could just walk the way the area car is pointing until I tell you to stop. OK, stop.

2. *If you go in the garden, to your right, it looks like your suspect is right up there by the bay window, by the bay window, you need to go into the garden, by into the garden, right up to the bay window. OK, if your colleague on the road can go up and cover the other section of the garden.*

3. *X Ray Sierra, please confirm that is your suspect. Thank you.*

1.

3.

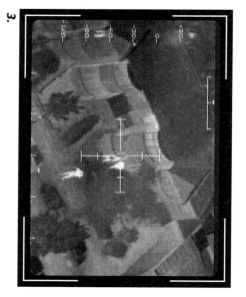

2.

HELICOP – FACTS

* Helicopters equipped with thermal imaging cameras are capable of detecting the body heat of someone swimming at 1000 m and of a person on land at 3000 m.
* New technology will soon allow police officers on the ground to receive live pictures directly from the helicopter on hand- held televisions.

Graffiti artists

At night, in crowded railway sidings, it was proving difficult to find two boys who had been reported spraying graffiti on wagons. But the helicopter, using its thermal imaging camera, which here shows heat as black, soon guided the officers on the ground to the culprits lying on top of a wagon.

MET AIR
SUPPORT UNIT

All the emergency services work closely together as this picture shows. From top to bottom: The AS 365 Dauphin Air Ambulance operated by HEMS in London, one of the Aerospatiale AS355N Twin Squirrels of the South East Region Police Air Support Unit, and a Bolkow 117CIC recently used in operational trials by the London Fire Brigade.

Blackpool fire

Emergency services are used to working closely together. On 16th August 1995 the police and fire brigade found themselves fighting this spreading fire in Blackpool close to the pleasure beach.

1. The Lancashire Police Helicopter Support Unit helicopter was able to assist the fire fighters by relaying pictures and commentary to a control room where senior fire and police officers coordinated the operation.

2. When the first fire tender had arrived, only five minutes after the initial 999 call, the fire fighters were confronted by a developing fire which had engulfed all three floors of a large retail building. The fire had started in a small stall in a shop which sold cheap butane cigarette lighters. When a few lighters caught fire, attempts to put out the growing flames by stamping on them only made the problem worse as the plastic cases burst, releasing more fuel into the fire.

3. Access to the building was made difficult by narrow streets and growing crowds. Parked cars were on fire and the surrounding buildings were at risk from the intense radiated heat.

4. The thermal image usually shows heat as white but can be switched to show particular temperatures in colour.

5. The helicopter spotted three overzealous members of the press within the evacuated area on the roof of a building at risk. Police officers on the ground were informed and they were moved to safety.

6. Using the thermal imaging camera, the helicopter could establish which buildings were most at risk. The burning embers, looking like a snowstorm on the thermal imaging camera, were settling and collecting in gulleys, creating new hot spots and additional fires.

1.

2.

3.

4.

7. The roof of this shop was registering as bright red on the camera, showing it close to burning. Without swift action it would have burst into flames.

8. With detailed information from the helicopter, the fire brigade were able to concentrate their hoses on the most vulnerable buildings.

9. Through the smoke and clouds of water vapour, the firemen on the ground could not see if the fire was totally under control, and the structure of the building was too unsafe for firemen to go in to check.

10. But the thermal imaging camera was able to verify the fire was out and the emergency was over.

11. This joint effort by the fire brigade and the police ensured the fire was subdued in less than three hours and without a single fatality. The only injured victims were two firemen who had minor burns on their feet caused by heat radiating through their boots.

Roof chase

A South East Region helicopter received an urgent call for help from ground forces at the British Museum in London. There had been an attempted break in and the helicopter team's skills were needed after one of the suspects had emerged on to the roof in an attempt to escape, followed by two police officers.

1.

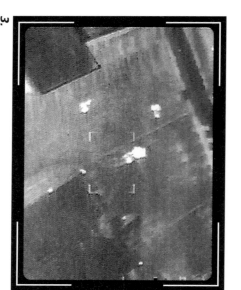

2.

3.

1. He tried to hide from them but he had not bargained for the thermal imaging camera's beady eye.

2. As the officers approached, he went on the run again, perilously close to the edge. The building was over 23 metres/75 feet off the ground. For the fugitive and his police pursuers, it was a high wire circus act without a net – one slip could have meant instant death.

3. The ground force lost sight of him, but the helicopter saw him disappearing through a skylight. With the information from the helicopter, police inside the building made the inevitable arrest.

4.

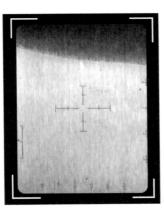

5.

6.

7.

Chiswick bridge

One December evening, just before midnight, the police received a 999 call from a drunk young man on his way home from a Christmas party with a group of friends. He told them that one of his friends had fallen into the Thames from West London's Chiswick Bridge – it was thought he had been trying to balance on a parapet. Ground forces were immediately sent to the scene, but there was no sign of the missing man.

4. The Air Support helicopter with its thermal imaging camera was already in the area and offered its help. Police officers on the ground considered the river currents and searched for the victim in the most likely area.

5. But the thermal image camera could find nothing. Fearing for his life in the icy waters, the search was widened to another area of the river and the camera suddenly picked up a very faint heat source close to the opposite bank. Using their powerful Night-sun floodlight, the helicopter crew guided the ground forces to the spot. As ground forces crossed the bridge, the heat source grew weaker as the man sank underwater. As he surfaced again, his image got stronger. He bobbed under the freezing water on two or three more occasions before an officer arrived at the water's edge expecting the worst.

6. The tide was out, making it easier for the policeman to pull the man from the river. The thermal image clearly showed how near to death this man was, his body registered as dark grey compared to the white heat of the policeman. The rescuing officers found that the man had a very faint pulse and was in an advanced stage of hypothermia.

7. Resuscitation procedures were started and he was wrapped in a foil blanket and carried by stretcher to a waiting ambulance. The hospital later confirmed that the man was only minutes away from death. His life was saved by the air support's expertise, the thermal imaging camera and the first aid administered by the ground forces. Air support units do not fly unless they have to, especially at night. Yet while this operation was taking place there were complaints about the noise of the helicopter even though the pilot and officers were just doing their job and, on this occasion, saving someone's life.

Highway
Video Patrol

'Police, Camera, Action!' also reports on the experiences of drivers and police officers around the world. It shows that Britain is far from being the only country in the world with a cavalier attitude towards road safety. Reckless driving is a common phenomenon world wide. And although the particular problems in specific countries can be different, they can also be pretty bizarre, with mysterious sights in some countries and downright dangerous driving in others.

In America, there are more cars per head of population than anywhere else in the world. It is a country that makes no apology for its love affair with the car, but bad driving in general is seen as less of a problem than that of driving under the influence of drugs or alcohol. In the US, video cameras are less likely to be running for the full duration of a patrol. Cameras are switched on 'at the officer's discretion' and used for specific evidence gathering in drug bust, drink driving and criminal pursuits.

The Californian Mystery Tour

There are an estimated 222 million firearms in circulation in the United States, so when the police pull someone over on the road, they just don't know if they will be facing a firearm. But some drivers don't need guns to behave as if they had a licence to kill. A huge luxury tour bus, weighing ten tonnes, and capable of carrying over 50 passengers, set off at 7pm, US Western time, from a coach station in San Diego with just one passenger aboard. The coach wasn't scheduled to leave the depot for another half an hour, but then this run wasn't on the timetable. The man driving was a hijacker.

Alerted by staff at the coach station, the police gave pursuit. Meanwhile, the lone passenger was let off – it turned out to be a ride he was glad to miss.

1. Driven without the use of its main headlights, the bus, tracked by helicopters and numerous police vehicles, left a trail of destruction in its wake. From San Diego to Burbank, through Malibu and on towards the San Fernando Valley it travelled.

2. At one point, the driver lost control and ended up going sideways. With the bus jackknifed in the road, the police hoped that it would be here on Sunset Boulevard, over 100 miles, and five hours on, from where the journey first began, that it would finally end. The driver, however, had other ideas.

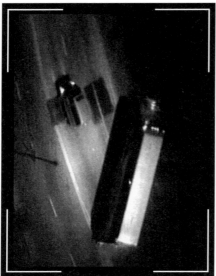

3. Sparks started flying when a chain link fence, caught up in the wheels, made contact with the road, the bus's progress was gruesomely illuminated in a shower of sparks. Hollywood locals must have felt they were suffering from *déjà vu*. They had already seen the film *Speed* at the cinema, but now its real life counterpart was being played out in their neighbourhood. This time, though, Keanu Reeves was nowhere to be seen. The bus finally took a wrong turn and was faced with a dead end street. With no way forwards and patrol cars behind it, the bus's driver still refused to surrender. He decided to reverse his way through the police vehicles.

3.

4.

4. Patrol cars were pushed around like toy cars so the officers responded by opening fire at the tyres. Determined to escape, the bus's only option was to try and turn round. Reversing straight into someone's living room, the bus was certainly an unwelcome guest at this household, but happily the owners were at the theatre that evening.

5. The end of the line came when the bus was surrounded and well covered by police marksmen. An officer attempted to smash open the driver's door. There was the ever-present fear that the hijacker may have been armed, so the police could afford to take no chances. They shot out the windows with hand guns to encourage the driver to give himself up. Eventually they managed to drag him from the cab without further damage. It turned out he had been refused a job by the bus company so he had decided to steal one instead. The driver gave his captors five different names and then refused to speak, which did not help matters. Eventually he was charged with ten counts of assault on officers, one count of vandalism and received psychiatric treatment while awaiting trial.

5.

SLEEPING POLICEMEN

In 1907, the Mayor of Glencoe, Illinois, introduced the radical technique of stretching steel cables across the roads to keep speeding automobiles out of his town. When he was sued for this rather dangerous practice, he had the roads dug up into artificial bumps – the very first use of 'sleeping policemen'.

Drunk Drivers

Alcohol-related traffic deaths are the single largest component of the total number of deaths on the roads in the United States. Police patrol cars collect the crucial evidence needed to convict drunk drivers in court, though few protest their innocence once they have seen themselves on tape. Most drunk drivers tend to give themselves away. Smelling a little, or often a lot, is as much of a problem in the United States as pretty well everywhere. Drink driving is a global scourge.

The Sobriety Test

Possible offenders face 'The Sobriety Test'. This is a series of simple tasks such as standing on one leg with your arms outstretched and counting to thirty, or touching your nose with your eyes closed. They aim to test coordination and concentration; easy if you are sober, a giveaway if you are drunk or drugged.

Failure leads inevitably, to the breathalyzer: if positive, it is the cuffs, the police station and an appointment with the doctor for a blood or urine test. At night, more than 70 percent of accidents involve a driver or a motorcyclist who has taken more than the legal level of alcohol.

HIGHWAY PATROL – A HISTORY

In 1935, America became the first country to equip patrol cars with a comprehensive range of equipment, two decades before Britain. Apart from an electric siren, compass, two spotlights, 10 ton hydraulic jack, crowbar, rope, grappling hook, fire extinguisher, public address system, two-way radio, blankets and stretcher, shovel, camera and flash, headlight testing equipment, stop meter for brake testing, detour and accident signs, tape and chalk, two flash-

lights, and a first aid kit, they also found room for flares, an automatic rifle, tear gas and gas masks, and a Thompson sub-machine gun.

The Tommy gun was mounted on the roof and fired using a foot switch through an opening in the wind shield. It was aimed by using a sight attached to the bonnet and lining up the car at the target.

It cost almost twice as much to equip the patrol car as it did to buy the car itself.

No messing about

1. With lives at stake, American police have no hesitation in damaging a patrol car if it succeeds in bringing a pursuit to a safe end.

2. In California, the Highway Patrol ended the pursuit of an armed man in a stolen car. The suspect slowed down, next to a wide driveway. It was the chance the police had been waiting for.

3. The police patrol car rammed the suspect's car down the driveway into a garage door, and the suspect was trapped.

4. Officers now approached the fugitive – the first one with a revolver, his partner covering him with a shot-gun. Wisely, the suspect surrendered and was made to lie, face down, on the ground. He was disarmed, handcuffed and arrested.

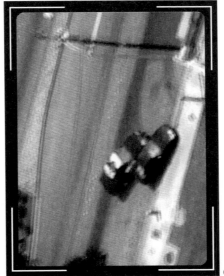

1.

2.

3.

4.

Coastguard

In the US, the battle against drugs is a well-coordinated operation between all the Law Enforcement Agencies including the Police, the FBI, the Drug Enforcement Agency and the Coastguard.

1. A Coastguard Falcon Aircraft, equipped with state-of-the-art thermal imaging cameras was following a cargo plane south of Jamaica. The Coastguard was suspicious because the plane's flight path was from Colombia, an obvious 'source' country, and it was keeping low over the ocean to avoid traffic control radar.

1.

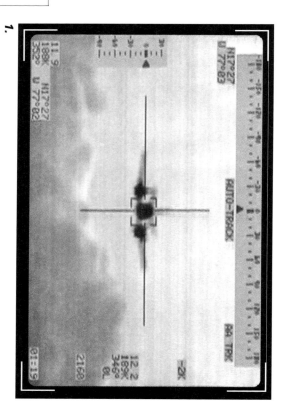

2.

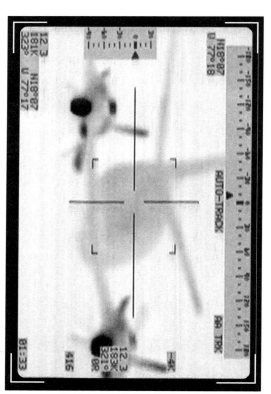

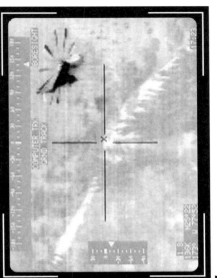

3.

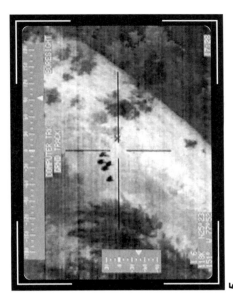

4.

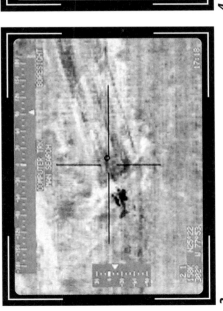

5.

2. But not even low cloud protected it as the Coastguard's camera tracked the aircraft.

3. The plane was observed right up to the moment it landed at Chub Quay in the Bahamas, and the Coastguard had already arranged a reception party.

4. Coastguard and army helicopters carrying Drug Enforcement Agents and Royal Bahamian Police officers surprised the suspects, who ran from their plane to find cover in the tall grass. But the deadly game was up.

5. Even at sunset, the suspects were easily spotted with the thermal image camera and quickly arrested. Meanwhile, the plane had been searched and found to be loaded with 635 kg/1400 lb of pure cocaine. The aeroplane and contraband were turned over to the Bahamian authorities and the smugglers prosecuted.

Armed and dangerous

There are many differences between policing in the States and in Britain. In Britain, the policy is to maintain a safe distance and work to stop the pursuit in a controlled manner. In the United States, they know a suspect is almost certainly armed. It is a sad truth in a society where guns are freely available, but it means the stakes are higher for both police and criminals, and there are often very good reasons for bringing a pursuit to a conclusion as quickly as possible.

This incident began one Wednesday morning in August 1994. The rain had made the driving conditions difficult as police chased an armed bank robber. He had sped off in a dark red car waving his gun at passing motorists. The police caught up with him, but it was a dangerous pursuit.

1. An officer leant out of the window, gun in hand. At this stage the target was the car tyres. In this situation the suspect had no chance of escape.

2. He was surrounded by police cars but, instead of giving himself up, he repeatedly pointed and fired his gun at the Minnesota State Patrol. Confronted with a suspect who was a lethal threat to the public and themselves, the police had to force the man off the road, as quickly as possible. The usual technique is 'fishtailing' – striking the rear of the bandit car to knock it sideways and out of control.

4.

6.

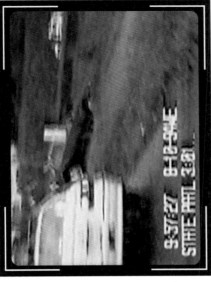

5.

7.

3. The officers in the black police car anticipated that the suspect would attempt to escape down the exit ramp.

4. – 7. The white patrol car blocked him off and forced him back onto the freeway. Before he could try to escape again, the patrol car behind him caught him with a fishtail and took him off the road.

The Patient State Trooper

Police in some parts of the United States have a reputation for sometimes being rather aggressive and rude. To prove this is not always the case, in Maine, the world's worst tempered driver was pulled over for speeding by the world's most patient State Trooper.

1. Irate driver: *Goddamn asshole. Now just gimme the goddamn ticket and let me get out of here. I didn't do nothing wrong, I know I didn't, now let me get the **** out of here. I ain't in no hurry but I had to get some pills for my dog. Just gimme that and get the **** out of here.*

2. State Trooper: *Can I just explain it to you, Sir, so you know what you'll need to do.*
Driver (shouting): *I know what to do, you're ripping me off and I didn't deserve it because I didn't do nothin' wrong. I thought it was a 40 mile zone whatever the frig it is. I never saw the sign, it said 55 mph and I was doing 57 and that's all, I know. Now just give me the goddamn thing and I'll look at the date and if I'm working I'll have to plead guilty if I've got to work because I can't afford to take the day off and if I'm not working I'll plead not guilty because I know damn well I'm not guilty. There. Now, are you State or Local? Looks like you're a State Trooper? So get back and pick up some more guys and run up the friggin' deficit on the working man. Just give me the goddamn thing and let me get out of here.*

3. State Trooper: *What you need to do is sign by the cross so that I can explain it to you. (He gives the driver the speeding ticket.)*
Driver: *I've got picked up for speeding before. You're guilty and you pay the fine and you try not to speed the next time and that's what I've been trying to do for the last 4-5 years before I ran into you — you asshole.*

4.

5.

4.

State Trooper: *The fine is right here sir, its* $137.50.

Driver (screaming): *You're ****in' crazy! Aaaah! Aaaah! You're ****in' crazy! Aaaah!* (He tears up the ticket and throws it away.)

State Trooper (quietly): *If you don't pick this up I'm going to summon you for litterin'.*

Driver: (screaming hysterically): *Are you ****in' crazy? Aaaaaaaaagh. I wasn't even speeding, you goddamn asshole. A hundred and thirty seven dollars? Aaagh!*

(But he picked up the pieces of ticket and got back in the car.)

4. State Trooper (even more quietly): *There's some more right there.*

5. Driver: *Aaaaaaargh!* (And he picks up the final piece of paper.)

6. Driver: *I never heard of a fine like that in my life you son of a bitch. You ****in' asshole. Let me get the **** out of here you goddam miserable ****. Jesus Christ!*

State Trooper (calmly as the vehicle disappears): *Bye.*

FLASHING POLICEMEN

The very first traffic lights in New York were fixed onto waistcoats worn by officers direct-ing traffic.

METERING OUT JUSTICE

The world's first parking meter was installed in Oklahoma City in 1935, but it was not until 1958 that they arrived in Britain. Appropriately, they were installed outside the American Embassy in London's Grosvenor Square.

6.

Motorway Madness

The expression 'motorway madness' has become a newspaperman's cliche to describe every major accident that happens. But from time to time there are incidents that range from the simply bizarre to the downright crazy.

The markings on police motorway patrol cars are deliberately designed to make them as conspicuous as possible. But just because an offending motorist cannot see a police car, it does not mean the driver is getting away with it. Most forces have unmarked video cars patrolling motorways and roads as well.

The car featured opposite is one such vehicle. This BMW 530i used by the Central Motorway Police Group, is typical of the high performance vehicles in use. With front and rear alternate strobing blue lights which are hidden until operated, there is nothing to make this car stand out from any other on the roads.

The sight of this 145 mph vehicle with blue lights flashing, coming up behind an unsuspecting motorist breaking the speed limit, can give quite a shock. No wonder it has been described as 'the best laxative known to man'!

Police — Help

The police are not there only to protect life and property, and to prevent crime, but to help us in any way they can. The motorway cameras have also recorded occasions when the traffic police do just that.

Tanker tow

1. The latest technological wizardry may make the police force's fight against crime more efficient, but there are times when a little old-fashioned improvization proves just as effective. Following an accident, an immobilized car blocked the overtaking lane on a motorway in Kent. It was a potential source of danger and disruption and the police were in a hurry to move it, but had no quick means of doing so. A passing tanker offered a solution. With a length of rope, a little ingenuity and plenty of pulling power, the car was towed to a more appropriate parking position.

Beating the drum

2. Traffic police are there to help as well as to enforce the law, and on this occasion they were even prepared to shift something that had fallen off the back of a lorry. When a large storage drum fell onto a motorway near Leatherhead, the driver got things right. Rather than trying to recover the load himself, he called to the police for assistance who helped remove the potential hazard. Further up the motorway, the police had slowed down the traffic to allow these officers to remove it safely.

3.

4.

5.

Overturned lorry

3. Something that is always a safe bet to provide the unexpected hazard to the British motorist is the British weather. A sudden strong wind blew this truck onto its side. Enlisting the support of a recovery vehicle, the police soon unblocked this Surrey motorway.

Slip-up

4. The driver who decided to do a three-point turn on this Hampshire motorway slip road was lucky to be interrupted by a very patient policeman, who persuaded her to turn back round and drive on to the next exit while he held up the traffic – and he did not even charge her.

The mobile kennel

5. The police spotted this dog travelling in style on a main road in North Wales. It can be perfectly safe and legal to tow a properly built trailer behind a motorbike, but as the current driving licence does not make this clear, there has been some confusion about the law.

Range Rover

Range Rovers and Discoveries are the workhorses of the motorway patrols. Although they have calibrated speedometers and can target speeding motorists, the amount of equipment they are able to carry allows them to play a much wider role.

Equipment fitted to vehicle

Red/blue strobe rooflights (red to rear only)

Front blue strobes

Alternate flashing lights front and rear

Whalen hi-lo/yelp/wail siren

Heavy duty front rubber nudge bars

Variable rear display sign

Calibrated speedometer

VHF radio

UHF radio

Tracker vehicle locator

Equipment carried but not shown in photo

Maglite torch

Tape measure

Seatbelt cutter

Evidence bags

Roadside phone 'Out of Service' hoods

Tachographic charts

Maps

Protective gloves

Stinger

8 traffic signs

An axe, hacksaw and crowbar

Tarpaulin

Wheelbrace

Tow rope   Shovel

1 gallon of water   Brush

12v 7kw Teklite floodlight

This Range Rover is operated by the Central Motorway Police Group at Perry Barr, and is one of the 18 police vehicles that patrol the 74 miles of motorway around Birmingham.

As well as front blue strobes and alternate flashing lights at the front and rear, it has red/blue strobe roof lights. The Whalen siren offers a choice of 'yelp', 'wail' or 'hi-lo', although the hi-lo is not used on the motorway as it is more suited to built-up areas. As well as the roof aerials for the UHF and VHF radios, the four centrally mounted aerials are connected to a Tracker locator unit used to trace stolen cars (see page 57).

There is also an LED rear display sign which can be programmed to show a range of messages from 'Police - Slow down', to a simple 'Thank you'. Heavy-duty rubber nudge bars at the front allow the crew to push instead of tow a broken-down vehicle off the carriageway.

First aid kit

Contamination/infection first aid kit

Resuscitator

Dry powder fire extinguisher

16 traffic cones

3 blue strobe cone lights

Slip Roads

Missing your turning off a motorway might be extremely aggravating, but the only thing to do is to continue to the next junction. It is when you try to rectify your mistake by taking a short cut that accidents can occur. Motorway cameras are constant witnesses to the chaos that this can cause.

Two-way traffic

1. The drivers in these cars, frustrated by the heavy traffic, decided to try to leave the motorway by reversing *en masse* up the hard shoulder to the junction. This type of dangerous driving is bad enough when the traffic is light, but with so many other cars on the road the situation quickly becomes confused.

2. But that was just the start. Twelve minutes later not only has the stream of traffic trying to get off the motorway grown, but the slip road is now blocked and almost as many cars are reversing down the slip road to join the motorway! Once they got to the scene the police were very fair – everyone got a ticket.

Death wish

3. This driver also missed his turning, so he stopped and pondered what to do – in the outside lane – for a good few minutes. He then hesitatingly crossed three lanes of on-coming traffic … and survived to make it onto the slip road. It would have been a stupid manoeuvre in dry conditions, let alone in the rain when on-coming traffic has even less chance of stopping in time.

Death wish 2

4. Both these drivers had taken a wrong turn, so they took their lives into their hands and reversed back along a slip road. But what happened next was almost unbelievable. One of the drivers decided to overtake the other in reverse – straight towards on-coming traffic. The police described this incident as 'suicidal impatience'.

4.

Death wish 3

5. Instead of leaving his broken down car on the hard shoulder, this driver had the not very bright idea of pushing it across the slip road. It meant that vehicles approaching at motorway speeds had to brake suddenly to avoid the blocked road.

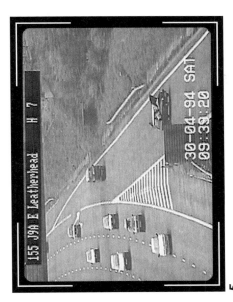

5.

Suicide driver

6. And this driver's actions amounted to near suicidal stupidity. Having missed his turning he decided to do a three-point turn on the motorway and drive back along the carriageway to the junction. With the road wet with rain, it was a manoeuvre that could have been a killer. Having nearly frightened himself and other motorists to death, the driver thankfully gave up on his plan and finally headed off in the right direction again until he could exit at the next junction.

LIFE FOR DEATH
A motorist who causes a fatal accident can be sentenced to life imprisonment if found guilty of Motor Manslaughter.

KEEPING DEATH OFF THE ROADS
In the 1930s in Beijing they did not bother with points on your licence - the penalty for speeding was death!

6.

Motorway Traffic

To ease the flow of traffic, there are restrictions on who and what can use motorways. But from time to time motorway cameras record users who should not be there.

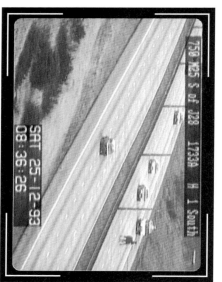

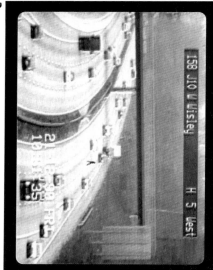

Motorway picnic

1. The motorcyclist on the right-hand side of the photograph had stopped for a cup of tea, and he was then joined by a lost motorist who has parked on the central reservation and crossed the road to ask for directions. It was not long before a traffic officer joined in the tea party, but the driver remained oblivious to the danger he had placed himself and others in. As the motorcyclist was unable to help, the driver even turned to the officer in the hope of guidance.

The loose horse

2. A fixed camera on the M25 recorded this stray reveller one Christmas morning. The horse had escaped from its more usual environment to go in search of fresh pasture. Galloping on and off the motorway, this marauding party animal was causing a danger not only to itself but also to Christmas travellers.

The motorway control room sent a patrol vehicle to encourage the animal back to its more usual habitat, but the attraction of high speed and danger was far more appealing and the horse resolutely refused to be rushed. Finally, with no concern for the hungry travellers it might have been keeping from their Christmas dinners, the horse decided to return to its field of its own accord.

The loose pedestrian

3. While we may do everything we can to avoid hurting animals, the drivers here were less sympathetic when this man crossed a busy motorway one Friday evening taking his life into his own hands …

4.

5.

6.

Hitch-hiker

4. ... as did this hitchhiker, yet another example of people putting their immediate needs before their own safety and the safety of others on the road. Thumbing a lift on the motorway is illegal for very good reasons. It is dangerous both for the hitch hiker and also for the cars that are forced to swerve or stop suddenly, making driving far more hazardous for others.

5. This impatient young man found out in the end that drivers won't stop if you try to bully them – until he got picked up by the patrol car despatched by the observer in the motorway control room.

Overtaking lane tyre change

6. These students had a flat tyre, but no jack. They tried to lift the car by hand to change the wheel. But as they had stopped in the overtaking lane, they were causing a serious hazard to themselves and other drivers. They clearly knew they should have pulled over to the hard shoulder, as one guiltily hopped over the barrier, and the other just tried to look innocent, when the inevitable police car arrived.

THE REAL M1?

The first stretch of motorway built in Britain was not the M1, as is commonly believed, but the Preston by-pass. Opened in 1957 and 8 1/4 miles long, it is now part of the M6. Today, Great Britain has 1,980 miles of motorway.

Danger – Drivers Ahead!

There are fewer deaths per mile on motorways than on other roads, but that does not mean they are safer. There may be no pedestrians, fewer and safer turnings and separated carriageways, but much higher speeds mean that one piece of stupidity or a lapse of concentration, can put not only yourself but many others at risk as well.

Porsche

1. Traffic police have a mixture of cars – some of them marked and some of them unmarked – so you won't always know when you are being followed. But as this driver's lack of reaction showed, some people would not even notice if the police had their sirens wailing and their blue lights flashing. In the bottom right-hand corner of the photograph, the Porsche was record-

ed as travelling at 145 mph. Travelling at this speed requires over 100 metres/350 feet to stop – that's about the length of three football pitches. Even when the police car flashed its headlights and switched on its blue lights, the driver took many miles to notice he was being followed. Don't forget, as the driver of this Porsche obviously did, that over 70 miles an hour on the motorway is too fast.

Perhaps the driver mistook the motorway for Brand's Hatch when he overtook the unmarked video patrol car on the inside.

Own goal

2. Motorway madness is not restricted to Britain. A driver in Japan was so proud of his new Ferrari, that he felt he just had to share its performance with others. The passenger seating of Ferrari sports cars being rather limited, he decided the best way to show it off was to make his own home video demonstrating its capabilities. And as he had the latest state-of-the-art gizmos on his camcorder he set up a second camera to record the speedometer in close-up as well.

Off he went down the motorway, 100 kilometres per hour ... 150 ... 200 ... 250 ... 300 ... 320 kph. On the right of the screen the speedometer is clearly showing 320 kph – nearly 200 mph.

But as the saying goes, pride comes before a fall. Our friend the video unwittingly provided the evidence for the driver's downfall. He was so proud of his achievement he made copies of the video available for sale to the public. But when a policeman happened to buy one, the driver was arrested and prosecuted for dangerous driving.

Ukrainian

3. Spotted doing a U-turn on a busy motorway, the Metropolitan Police were more than a little baffled as to what this white car was trying to achieve.

3.

4. As the driver emerged and headed towards the cones, they wondered whether he might be from the Government's Cone Hot Line on an unofficial check.

4.

5. His true intention, incredible as it might seem, became clear as he made a path through the cones large enough for a car to pass through. Fed up with the slow pace of traffic in the direction he was travelling, the driver had chosen to abandon any notion of good sense and attempted to join the other carriageway. The fact that the cones were there as a warning and deterrent were simply ignored.

Once through, the driver had to negotiate a perilous re-entry into the traffic flow – made especially dangerous because, of course, he had to join the fast moving traffic in the outside lane. When the driver was later pulled over by police, he explained he had no idea that his manoeuvre was illegal and hadn't realised what the cones indicated. But then it was his first trip to Britain from the Ukraine.

5.

The Liver Run

A t the Cromwell Hospital in London in May 1987, a transplant patient's body was chronically rejecting her recently replaced liver. A nationwide search located a suitable donor organ in Hull, and so began a life or death race against time to bring that organ to London. But the problems began immediately.

First the plane arranged to fly the transplant organ to London was delayed by thick fog. The ambulance service found itself unable to provide a vehicle that could do the journey to the hospital in time, and the Metropolitan Police Air Support Unit helicopter was grounded because of a technical problem.

Two cars of the No. 2 Area Traffic Unit of the Metropolitan Police Traffic Unit based at Chadwell Heath were given the important task of completing the last vital stage in this journey. They had just 35 minutes to cover the 29 miles across central London on a busy Friday afternoon. And that journey became the subject of a 'Police, Camera, Action!' special.

Patrol cars are kept in tip-top condition to minimize the risk of breakdown. But in an emergency situation like this, when anything could happen, a back-up car is there to take over. This time the back-up car was equipped with one of the first in-car video units in Britain.

When the 'Police, Camera, Action!' programme about 'The Liver Run' was being made, Aliza Hillel, right, who was the recipient of the donated liver, had the opportunity of meeting and thanking the two officers who saved her life. PC Bill McIntyre on the far right drove the lead car and PC Graham Fordham was his co-driver.

The Great Dash

1.

2.

Our story began at five minutes before midday at junction 7 on the M11 motorway on the outskirts of London. The Metropolitan Police officers were anxiously waiting to collect the liver from the Essex Police who had fetched it from Stansted Airport.

PC Graham Fordham, the co-driver of the car carrying the liver, takes up the story. *'We'd been having a refreshment break and were suddenly told that the aircraft had taken off from Hull and was due at Stansted within a matter of minutes, so it was a case of drop everything, leave the breakfast, and just go.'*

PC Les Crossland was driver of the backup car. *'The Essex car had gone onto the runway at Stansted Airport which was junction 8 and they'd run alongside the aircraft to pick up the package.'*

PC Bill McIntyre drove the lead car: *'We saw the Essex Police car coming down the M11, we moved forward, they drew in behind us and we transferred the organ from their car to our car.'*

Graham Fordham: *It took me by surprise when I went to make the changeover from the Essex Police car and I realised that it was a very large picnic box. On most organ runs you expect to find stainless steel containers.*

1. Human organs can only last for a certain number of minutes depending on what that organ is. At that time a liver could last for about 12 hours, and the delays meant that it only had about 30 minutes before it deteriorated too much to be used.

PC Bill McIntyre: *We were told that the liver had to be delivered to the hospital at 12.30pm. As we began to move off, I looked at the clock in the car and it was 11.56am. I began to wonder whether we had enough time in which to carry out our run.*

Time was the crucial factor in the journey. The clock at the top right-hand corner of the pictures shows the actual time ticking by. The speed is shown, as usual, at the bottom right-hand corner.

2. The first section of the journey was the M11 motorway and to keep on schedule they had to cover 27 miles in just 33 minutes.

3. PC Les Crossland: *As soon as we hit the M11 southbound we were confronted with roadworks. It was down to two lanes and a lorry pulled out in front of us. And that's even with two police cars, headlights, blue lights, sirens, wailers and still this lorry driver just stayed out there. I presume he didn't realise what was going on and, of course, that caused a little bit of frustration because we had to average about 60 mph from start to finish and this should have been relatively the easy part of it, where we could actually gain on time.*

3.

4. PC Bill McIntyre: *We were travelling at speeds of up to 120 mph on the motorway travelling towards London. Not the kind of speed we travel at every day and certainly not to be recommended to anyone to try, but then again our training shows us that we can be capable of this. Only in exceptional circumstances would we use these high speeds and this was a very exceptional circumstance.*

At the end of the motorway, the cars entered the East End of London. There were 26 minutes remaining and they had 15 miles still to cover. Although their route had been carefully planned, they had no idea what problems they could expect up ahead, or even if they could possibly make it in time.

PC Les Crossland: *We knew where we had to finish up and we'd planned a route which was acceptable to Scotland Yard bearing in mind they knew the traffic flow and conditions. And then when we were sitting at junction 7 and had picked the route and subject to us being told to change routes that was the one we were going to stick at. I think Graham had an A to Z in the front and certainly Steve who was with me in the video car behind, he had an A to Z.*

4.

5. At the first set of traffic lights the first congestion caught them. They wormed their way through, but their speed was down to about two miles an hour. As they got further into London, 13 miles away from the hospital, they moved into more residential areas. The streets become narrower and busier. It is not just other drivers that the police are worried about. The safety of pedestrians becomes a major concern.

6. PC Les Crossland: *It really got difficult when we went down High Road Leytonstone because I took the wrong side of the road and I think I stayed there; we were doing over 50 down there. I had the wailer going and I think that Bill had the yelper going trying to inform the public that there were two police vehicles coming through.*

I wasn't particularly concerned about the liver because I genuinely thought it would be packed in ice or even another container and that the cool box was just a means of transportation. What I didn't know was that Graham was leaning over into the back seat holding the lid down for the whole of the journey. So that came as a bit of a shock. It must have been a bit of a strain for him because he also had to give a radio commentary as well.

PC Graham Fordham: *I was quite fearful that had I taken my hand off the lid we would have had the contents of the box all over the back of the car*

and that would have rather brought the escort to an abrupt halt.

Any damage to organs during transportation is unlikely as they are very carefully packed. But they have a limited life outside the human body, however well they've been prepared.

Deterioration can be slowed down but not stopped, so every second counts. The police officers reached 60 mph on this part of the journey, knowing that every minute they gained meant an increased chance of survival for the patient.

PC Bill McIntyre: *Throughout the journey we did not give up hope at all but the one thought in your mind all the time is that someone's life is depending on what you are doing.*

At twelve minutes past twelve the police were still on the outskirts of London. They knew they only had 18 minutes to travel 8 miles to the hospital.

PC Les Crossland: *12.30 was the critical time and we were told in no uncertain terms that if we weren't there by 12.30 we were to abort the run.*

It was then they hit the traffic.

PC Bill McIntyre: *It was a Friday and lunchtime. We had to travel through the East End of London, the City, the West End of London, to reach the hospital.*

PC Les Crossland: *To think you've got to go through London at around about rush hour time or dinner time didn't exactly appeal to me but there was no other way round it. So I knew we had plenty of help in front of us. I knew we had the majority of junctions covered because the new command complex at New Scotland Yard had just opened up and really I think this was a good test for it.*

Because the route was planned through Scotland Yard they were able to notify local stations and traffic units that they needed assistance through traffic lights, junctions and roundabouts.

7. PC Bill McIntyre: *We had a great deal of assistance, the organisation worked, and a number of the junctions were manned so that we could have a clear run through.*

PC Les Crossland: *I think if you look at the entire run, something like 51 police officers took part in it.*

The co-driver in the lead car was in constant radio contact with Scotland Yard to inform them of their whereabouts and the traffic conditions. These updates were vital if the drivers needed assistance on the way and, with 7 miles to travel in 16 minutes, they wanted all the help they could get.

In spite of blue flashing lights and wailing sirens, some motorists still seemed unaware of the urgency of the situation. A clear path through the traffic could have been the difference between life and death.

Just 15 minutes before they were due at hospital, and with six miles still to go, the patrol cars were joined by two solo motorcyclists from the City of London Police tried to help them get through the crowded City. Riding way up ahead, they did their best to warn traffic and pedestrians that an emergency escort was under way. Any time saved at that stage of the journey could have proved crucial.

7.

8. PC Bill McIntyre: *Most drivers moved over to their near side whenever they saw the police car coming up behind them with the blues lights flashing. The exception was a red car which moved in front of my car, but if you look closely at it you can see that the red car has German number plates and that the driver of that car was actually obeying the rules of the road for their own country.*

We knew nothing at all about the recipient of the liver. We didn't know who the person was – male, female, adult, or child. But you still have the responsibility to try and get the organ to the hospital as quickly as you can because someone's life depends on it … and that is the motivation behind you, as it were.

9. PC Les Crossland: *It's something I've never done before. It's the first for me and it is not something that I would relish because obviously you know somebody is critical in a hospital, and someone will, of course, have died so there's no pleasure in it.*

The patient had, in fact, already undergone one transplant operation but her body was chronically rejecting the new liver. This second replacement liver was vital for her survival. Before the donor organ left the Hull hospital, a medical team had already assessed its suitability and the operation was started on the assumption

it would arrive on time. Without a new liver there would have been no chance of survival.

At speeds of over 50 mph through the City, the police were making better progress, but there were still five miles to travel in just 13 minutes through London's busy West End – it did not look good.

PC Bill McIntyre: *As we drove along the Embankment we were told over the radio by our control room that they had been in touch with the hospital and told them to expect us within 10 minutes. I looked at my watch, checked the time and thought 'Oh dear'.*

The hospital were relying on the officers arriving within an allotted time. The police had to tread a fine line between safety and speed. But they now knew more than ever that someone's life was depending on them, and they might not be able to make it in time.

PC Les Crossland: *When we were going along the Embankment we got called up to say that the hospital had obviously asked where we were and an ETA of 10 minutes had been given and I think Steve said to me, 'Oh they will have started the operation by now because when we get there I think it's just a straight*

10.

11.

transplant in', and I was aware in my own mind that if we didn't get there the person would die.

From the Embankment, there was four miles to cover and with the average speed of London traffic down to just 10 miles an hour, time was running out.

The patrol cars drove up Northumberland Avenue towards Trafalgar Square where the police had cleared a route through to the Mall. This is the very heart of London and filled with tourists. But these drivers had no time to admire the sights.

10. PC Les Crossland: *When we went down the Mall we had two City of London solo riders who were brilliant they were. In fact, I think one of them actually packed up motor cycling afterwards he was so exhausted from that. It may not seem much to you if you look at it. His bike, in fact, packed up, but you can see large plumes of smoke coming from the rear of it.*

11. PC Les Crossland: *And then when we went up through Constitution Hill, we came to Hyde Park Corner and Steve said to me you can go straight over here and lo and behold we did go straight over and so again that saved valuable time.*

The police still faced the daunting task of travelling three miles through the busy streets of Kensington before they could even think of reaching the hospital.

PC Les Crossland: *We then got diverted. Our original plan was to go through Knightsbridge and we got diverted down South Carriage Row because of traffic congestion and along there, that's when I was basically follow the leader, I didn't know where we were going. I wasn't too familiar over there.*

For these police officers, whose duties usually kept them on the outskirts of London, these roads were unfamiliar. They rarely venture into the centre of London. However, the long straight road through Hyde Park was a blessing. And, with only eight minutes to go, a stretch with speeds of over 60 mph just might just be what they needed to get them to the hospital in time.

PC Bill McIntyre: *Obviously, if you are driving at high speeds and having to brake at those speeds then your brake pads can get very hot and there were a couple of occasions when we could smell a burning smell coming from the wheels.*

12.

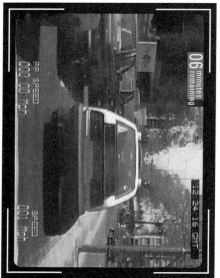

13.

14.

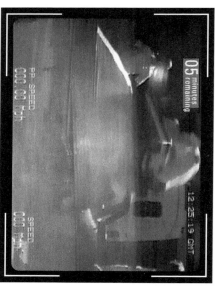

12. PC Bill McIntyre: As we turned into the Cromwell Road and the final approach to the hospital we were very much on our own, especially when crossing over the junctions. It was very much a case of trying to make as much progress as we could without inconveniencing other road users. But, of course, again trying to go against the clock.

The hospital was now less than a mile away and the police had covered one mile every minute – a remarkable average speed of 60 mph. But it was not over yet. They were in the heart of an area of London notorious for regular traffic gridlocks. Even when they arrived outside the hospital there was one more problem to overcome.

13. PC Les Crossland: I didn't actually know we were at the hospital. All I saw was Bill put a right-hand signal on and thought this doesn't seem a particularly main road. And as we turned in to – I don't know the name of the road – just alongside the hospital, because of traffic congestion there was somebody sat there blocking the entrance to the hospital. I think that out of all of it if I was going to say the wrong words it would have been then, to that motorist then.

14. The cars turned into the hospital at 12.25pm. They had made it with five minutes to spare.

PC Les Crossland: I felt really chuffed. I knew we'd done our bit and now it was down to the surgeon and the hospital staff.

15. It was all worthwhile; the patient survived. Aliza Hillel has now completely recovered from her operation. It has transformed her life and her family's. And until 'Police, Camera, Action!' showed her the race against time across London, she was quite unaware of the effort that had gone into getting her new liver to the hospital.

15.

BLUE LIGHT RUN

When the emergency services use their blue lights on their way to an incident, with or without the sirens, they call it a 'Blue light run'. If you are driving along minding your own business, it can be an unsettling experience when a police car or fire engine comes up behind you with strobes flashing and sirens blaring. Some drivers freeze, stopping dead in the middle of the road and creating an obstacle for the police to negotiate, others panic and swerve into the path of the emergency vehicle. To avoid causing problems, remember these tips:

• Do not be panicked by the speed and noise of the emergency vehicles

• Do not stop dead in the middle of the road

• Check the position of other vehicles on the road - is the path ahead clear?

• If you are next to a cycle lane, look out for cyclists.

• Slow down and make room for the emergency vehicle to pass, only pulling over to the side of the road and stopping if neccessary

• Do not pull over on the brow of a hill or a corner and do not go onto the pavement

• Be careful if you are approaching or are at a road junction

• Be aware of pedestrians - especially if you are near traffic lights or a school

Eurocops

An increasing number of European countries are recognising that video is a useful weapon in the war against bad drivers.

As we have seen, America has its own way of using police video, but in mainland Europe the way that video is employed is much the same as in Britain. Nevertheless, each country has its own peculiar problems, and they cover a much wider range of traffic violations. In the Scandinavian countries, their winters provide particular problems; in Holland, cycling is a cheap, popular and environmentally friendly means of transport, but it is not necessarily that safe; and in Germany, they treat Autobahns like racing circuits.

Every two years police officers and patrol vehicles from all over Europe gather together for the European Police Festival. The third festival, held in London in 1994, saw representatives from over thirty forces arriving from as far afield as Latvia and Romania. Combined with the Chigwell Show, the Metropolitan Police's premier public event, it gave the public an opportunity to discover how different police forces operate, and for the officers to exchange views and ideas.

Europe's finest at the 1994 European Police Festival in Chigwell.

No Limits

One of the most important techniques the police use is what is known in the US as the 'Cell of Safety'. This is a system where the driver keeps a cocoon of space around the car, allowing the officer enough time and space to carry out any emergency procedure.

In part, it is simply common sense, but it is something that a lot of drivers fail to understand, particularly on some of the high-speed motorways in mainland Europe.

Lorries tailgating
1. Whatever the Polish for 'braking distance' is, these drivers near Warsaw do not seem to have heard of it.

Overtaking ...
2. And this over-taking lorry-driver seems to have a suicide pact with the other road users.

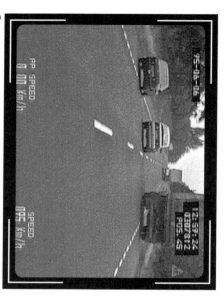

... and double overtaking
3. Yes, this is a single carriageway. That the Mercedes driver should use the hard shoulder on the *other* side of the road for a double overtake defies belief. But there was more.

4. The Mercedes driver continued to dice with death, staying on the wrong side of the road almost to the brow of the hill.

6.

5.

Belt up

5. Seat belt laws now are common throughout Europe, but some countries are more rigorous than others in enforcing them. It is illegal for children to travel in the front seat in most European countries whether secured or not. Seeing this small boy in Holland having to steady himself by pressing his hand on the dashboard while the car slows down, indicates that the dangers are obvious.

6. With traffic lights ahead and the road wet with rain, the driver of this white car in Holland was allowing plenty of time to stop safely. But if he had to break suddenly, it is not hard to imagine what the consequences could have been for this child unsecured in the front seat. The car was pulled over and the driver was prosecuted.

Cover up

7. For some reason, street behaviour is often more bizarre in Europe than in Britain. Danish Police discovered this militant naturist. She had already attracted the attentions of a passing cyclist but seemed determined to ignore the remonstrations of both her and her own friend who is tagging along behind. It resulted in a police cover-up but, in this case, it was the only decent thing to do!

BELT UP

The first patent for seat belts was taken out in Paris in 1903 by inventor Gustave Lebeau, who described them as 'protective suspenders for automobiles and other vehicles'. It was 1991, 88 years later, before seat belt wearing became law for all car drivers and passengers in Britain.

7.

The car in front is ...

... a Toyota

1. And this pick-up truck was determined to stay there. In Copenhagen, the police were in pursuit of a stolen blue pick-up. The driver headed out of town and on to the motorway. This was exactly what the officers wanted as it removed the bandit vehicle from the crowded city streets and made the pursuit more controllable.

2. The longer the chase continued, more and more police cars joined in the operation to stop it. In spite of the risks, the police tried to get in front – but the thief had other ideas.

3. In common with British practice, the Danish police manoeuvred their cars to box in the pick-up. At such high speeds and with determined criminals, this is a very dangerous practice.

4. At one point, they almost had the fugitive boxed into the outside lane. But he just managed to squeeze out of the trap by using the central reservation.

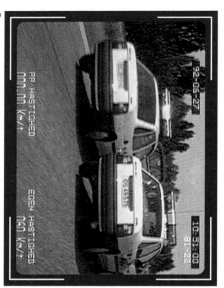

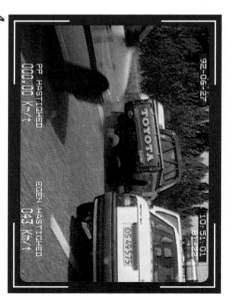

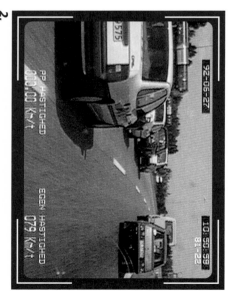

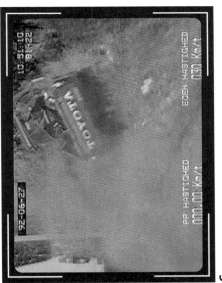

5.

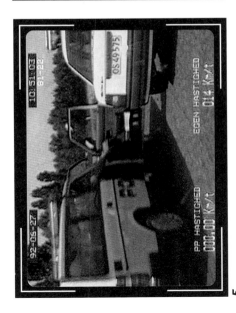

6.

7.

8.

5. In the hurry to continue the chase, one of the patrol cars tried to take the door of another police car with it.

6+7. But the Toyota had damaged its steering while pushing out of the trap and shot off the road into a road sign. This was not the controlled stop the police had planned, but luckily no one was hurt.

8. Ice skating

With the sub-zero temperatures in Scandinavia, even experienced ice drivers can get caught out. This may look like something from *Holiday on Ice*, but as we know from our own winters, ice can be deadly serious. With speeds of over 60 kph (37mph), this Swedish driver was very lucky to avoid a major crash.

Autobahn

Germany's autobahns have no maximum speed limit but they do know about dangerous driving. Although there is a recommended maximum of 130 kph (just over 80 mph), the average speed is over 150 kph (95 mph), and as anyone who has driven on an autobahn will tell you, many drivers drive a good deal faster than that. High-speed tailgating is far more common than in Britain, as these pictures show.

1.

2.

3.

4.

1. In these shots, the two horizontal white lines on the carriageway represent what German police judge to be the minimum braking distance between two cars.

2. These four drivers squeezed together in the Safety Cell think they know better. But as they bunch together, the puff of smoke from screeching tyres of the second car shows how close they came to catastrophe. Notice, too, how the crane-driver had to beat a hasty retreat to the hard shoulder to avert another tragedy.

3. In Germany, the motorway speed limits may be more liberal, but penalties for dangerous driving are more severe. The driver of the tailgating white car was fined £550 and had his licence suspended for a month.

4. Look at the car behind the two lorries at the top of the picture. The hard shoulder is for emergencies, not overtaking. Trying to turn a two-lane highway into a three-laner cost this driver a £700 fine and a two month ban.

Dangerous Euroloads

While there are particular problems with cyclists in the Netherlands, and with high-speed motorway driving in Germany, there are some habits which drivers in every European country are equally guilty of - such as badly or overloaded vehicles!

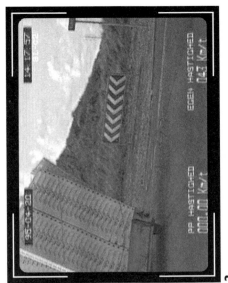

1.

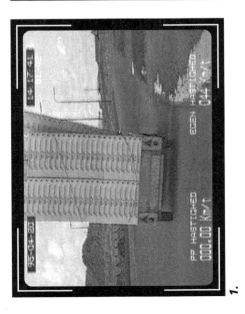

3.

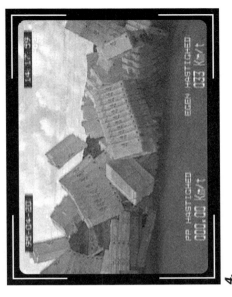

2.

4.

A matter of timing

1- 4. And the question about this optimistic farmer's sky high load was not would it?, but when?

EURO FACTS

In Britain, vehicles are driven on the left of the road, but most other countries drive on the right. In Italy, up to 1923, they had the worst of both worlds as they had to drive on the left in towns, and on the right in the country!

He's a lumberjack?

1. This log, casually put on the back of the truck, measured more than 6 metres/20 feet with virtually nothing to tie it down.

Car on a stick

2. When this driver loaded the length of wood into his car he thought there was plenty of room. But he forgot about little things like road signs and other road users.

The power of the press?

3. And this travelling roof was not attached to the lorry at all. The driver seemed to believe a rolled-up newspaper and the force of gravity would keep other road users safe.

The power of prayer

4. Here, two spare tyres and a prayer were all that kept this mobile home from joining the rest of the traffic – it is not attached to the truck at all.

6.

5.

Overload

5. When the Dutch police were overtaken by a car literally crammed full of children, they were a little bemused. There were so many it was impossible to count them and it was only the number of cycles being towed that gave it away - incredibly it was nine in all.

Three up

6. Somehow these three Dutch teenagers have all managed to get on this moped but it is anyone's guess how long they will all be able to stay on.

EUROSPEED FACTS

In 1900, France was the first country to use photography to catch vehicles breaking the speed limit. Like modern systems, it took two timed exposures of the moving object. Unlike modern systems, it worked well with a horse and carriage, but because of the slow shutter speeds then used, it could not cope with the fast moving automobiles.

In Germany at the turn of the century, they decided that the way to control speeding motorists was for cars to have a large visual speed indicator on the outside of every car. Unfortunately, tests showed that the faster the car went, the less accurate the indicators were. In the end they decided on the same speed control system as in Britain – policemen with stop watches!

The Spanish first introduced regular roadworthiness tests for cars in 1901. Britain did not introduce them until 1960.

The world's first motorway was in Italy between Milan and Varese. It was 13 miles long and opened in September 1924. Within nine years, Italy had built 12,500 miles of special motor roads.

Bike Behaviour

The Dutch have the widest network of cycle lanes in Europe and their Highway Code was specifically designed with the cyclist in mind. But no matter how many rules and regulations you have, the cyclist remains a vulnerable road user. As the pictures from Dutch police video recordings demonstrate, they are not only at the mercy of motorists, they are also just as likely to put their own lives at risk!

In Holland, traffic related deaths are amongst the lowest in Europe but it is something they have had to work at really hard to achieve. Road safety is a recognised part of the school curriculum and Dutch kids are a lot more safety conscious. But as the pictures from a clip that we have discovered show, it is often the adults who really need educating.

Unsafe hands

1. Although this child has been securely strapped in to her seat and is wearing a crash helmet, her father, peddling purposefully on his way home, is quite unaware his daughter keeps nodding off, and that her hand is dangling perilously close to the spokes of the back wheel of the bicycle.

A close call

2. The cyclist had a narrow escape, but the driver was not so lucky with a police video recording of his driving!

Drunk in charge

3. In his drunken state, if this man had ever managed to get on his bike, it would have been a miracle, let alone being able to ride it. Even with the whole bike lane to himself, he still managed to wobble onto the pavement and intimidate pedestrians.

A small mistake

4. Minis may be small, but they certainly don't have two wheels, so this car should not be using this cycle lane in Holland.

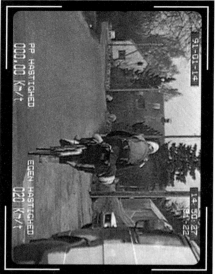

1.

2.

3.

4.

5.

6.

Cycling pirate?

5. Nor should this boat – or is it a boat? It certainly has a sail, but on further investigation police discovered this ingenious contraption was carefully designed so that the cyclist, who had a wooden leg, could balance on his two wheels effectively.

Underpowered

6. And how was this boat managing to move? As they drew up alongside, at first the police could not see, but when it became clear, they could not quite believe it.

FAST AND FURIOUS

Speeding cyclists are subject to far more punishing penalties than speeding motorists. As well as having to comply with speed limits, under an act dating back to 1835, a cyclist found guilty of 'furious riding' can be sentenced to two years in prison and an unlimited fine!

Pursuits

Stolen vehicles are habitually used by armed robbers, terrorists and violent offenders. When a vehicle suddenly bolts away from a police car, officers generally have no idea what kind of criminals they are dealing with, or the level of threat they pose to the public.

Motorways bear witness to a lot of inconsiderate driving but they are also a favourite escape route for criminals as well. These sequences show just how careful police patrols have to be, not only to catch the criminals, but also to protect other road users.

It has been thirty years since police forces started to make patrol cars more conspicuous by using a design of white with fluorescent red stripes, rather than simply painting them black or blue. But the designs have always followed the lines of the vehicle, and have been based on subjective, rather than scientific, grounds.

However, the very latest markings, which are now beginning to be seen on Britain's roads, are based on detailed research work carried out by the Police Scientific Development Branch.

Red and white are out as blue and yellow have been found to be the most conspicuous combination. And instead of stripes, it has been discovered that a chequered pattern significantly improves visibility. Unsurprisingly, the new colours are already unofficially known as 'Battenburg' markings.

Black BMW

When the police are involved in a pursuit, they always follow a plan, and that plan will never deliberately involve a member of the public. Such situations are considered far too dangerous for anyone who has not had the appropriate training and trying to help from a position of ignorance can only make things worse.

1. This stolen black BMW was heading south from Birmingham at 130 mph followed by a patrol car. The driver showed no sign of stopping and the police were prepared to follow him all the way to London if necessary. But on this occasion they did not need to. The help they received from two members of the public proved very useful in bringing the pursuit to an end.

2. The driver of the white car slowed down when he saw the BMW and a police car approaching from behind, forcing the BMW following to do the

1.

2.

3.

SPEED LIMITS

- **1896** Limit of 12 mph imposed on all roads
- **1903** Speed limit raised to 20 mph
- **1935** 20 mph limit abolished, but 30 mph limit on urban roads introduced
- **1965** Introduction of 50 mph limit on 500 miles of roads
- **1967** An overall 70 mph limit imposed on all roads and motorways.

same. But after the fugitive started nudging his bumper, he decided he had had enough and moved onto the hard shoulder.

3. Further up the road, a blue van tried the same thing and was more successful. The driver realised what was going on, and having slowed down the BMW he moved neatly out of the way, allowing two patrol cars to pincer the front of the bandit car.

4. The police weren't able to thank the driver of the blue van as he didn't stop and no record was made of his number plate, but they would like him to know that they were extremely grateful.

Dangerous or reckless driving could land you with a fine, a ban or even a prison sentence. More seriously, you could critically injure or kill yourself or an innocent road user.

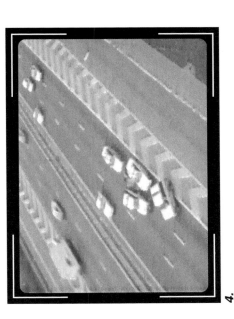

4.

STINGER

Tyre deflating devices have been around for a long time. The basic idea is obvious, but many of the designs were unsophisticated and not very easy to operate, so they had never entered general use with police forces. Stinger changed all that, and is now often carried as part of the standard equipment for police vehicles in Britain. In a pursuit, the police control room, which will be in contact with all the cars in the area, will arrange for a Stinger unit to be deployed ahead of the target vehicle. It is designed to stop all kinds of speeding and stolen vehicles by a controlled, and therefore safe, deflation of the tyres. An extendable trellis of hollow steel spikes is thrown or pulled across the road. As the target vehicle passes over the spikes they detach themselves, and as the wheel turns, the spikes in the tyre come into contact with the road driving them fully into the tyres. The tyres deflate and the vehicle comes to rest - for example, a car travelling at 100 mph will slow down to 15 mph in just 6 seconds. In the meantime, the officer operating the Stinger can pull it back off the road and out of the way of any following vehicle. Stinger can bring a swift and safe end to the most dangerous driving.

Red Astra

Police pursuit technique includes a non-stop running commentary as events unfold. In this sequence of pictures, notice the precision and control of the police driver as he maintained a safe distance from the criminal's car. The police driver's commentary not only informed his colleagues in the vicinity of the criminal's exact location, but also recorded every driving offence committed. When this case came to court, the criminals were judged not only for the theft of the vehicle but also for numerous counts of dangerous driving.

Police video like this provides absolute proof in court. With this kind of evidence, a defence lawyer would find it difficult to play down the seriousness of the offences or to argue for provocation by the police.

This is the commentary recorded on the video when a red Astra Gti failed to stop when requested:

The commentary

Tango Romeo 35. Red Astra Gti. Failure to stop. Three up. Vehicle failing to stop.

1. Three four zero, approaching right-hand bend. Going for an overtake.

2. 80 mph. Approaching Tidmarsh, through Tidmarsh Village, 40 mph speed limit ahead. 85 mph. Braking, braking, braking. Reducing speed to 40 mph. Going left, left, left. Back way to Tilehurst.

3. Left-hand blind bend. 50mph. This is being recorded on video.

4. Coming up behind a white Marina van. It's going for the overtake, approaching go slow signs. Left-hand bend. No reduction in speed, almost took out a blue Peugeot approaching Nunpipe Lane on the right-hand side, accelerating.

3.

4.

5.

6.

5. *Approaching two pedestrians on the footpath, accelerating to 60 mph.*
Solemn Hill towards Tilehurst, 35 mph, right-hand bend.
Accelerating hard, 50 mph.
Across the central white line approaching on-coming vehicle.
Wrong side of the road for right-hand bend. Going right, braking hard.
Sharp right bend, over the central white line. Left-hand bend.
Braking, braking, braking. Towards Purley. Long lane towards Purley.
Accelerating hard, 50 mph. Confirm three occupants.
Braking hard. Right-hand bend.

6. *Snaking over the road. Vehicles ahead. 40 mph speed limit, doing 65 mph.*
Passing junction.
Braking hard. Right-hand bend.
Blue lights activated. Two tones on. Still no response. Failure to stop. Right-hand
bend. Crossing the white lines.
Continued overleaf

7.

9.

8.

10.

7. *Approaching the traffic light junction. Roadwork sign ahead. Red traffic lights, through the lights going left, left, left, onto the A329.*

8. *Approaching roadworks, going straight on approaching slow moving queue of traffic. 40 mph speed limit. We're doing fifty.*

9. *Indicating to go left. Get ready for a decamp. Into the bus lane.*

10. *Go alongside, John, alongside. Vehicle stopping. Decamp.*

The ending was as you would expect – the criminals finally realised the inevitability of their capture and gave themselves up.

Car crime

Car crime makes up a third of all reported crime in the UK. Three out of four thefts from cars take place in the evening or at night. Over half of all thefts are from cars parked at the owner's home. Some 96 percent of stolen vehicles fitted with the latest tracking devices are found within five hours.

Off-road Range Rover Pursuit

It is not just the roads and motorways that are the domain of the traffic police. The great advantage of helicopters is that they can go where cars can't. And no matter how hard you try, you just can't get away – as the drivers of this stolen Range Rover were to discover.

1. It is not quite as easy as it seems to avoid capture when being pursued by the most sophisticated of police surveillance vehicles. While the drivers might think they can escape from their pursuers on the ground, by driving through a hedge into a field, they are never without the company of the helicopter. The helicopter was able to maintain constant communication with the police on the ground and every move the drivers made was tracked and recorded for evidence. And for anyone still wondering how crop circles come about, this is perhaps as good an answer as any.

2. When the Range Rover finally came to rest in the hedgerow, the helicopter crew maintained surveillance and continued to direct their colleagues.

3. Through a combined effort between the helicopter, the police on the ground and that most useful of police tools, the Alsatian, the culprits were eventually forced to give themselves up.

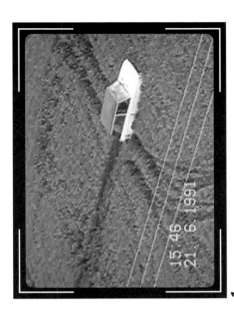

15:46
21. 6. 1991

1.

15:47
21. 6. 1991

2.

15:48
21. 6. 1991

3.

M25 Red and White Van Pursuit

Video cars can provide essential evidence for the police, not only in their war against reckless driving, but also in the prosecution of other criminals. Refusing to stop only makes things worse and reckless driving can incur serious penalties – even a prison sentence.

1. A police car was called to join the pursuit of a red and white van on the M25. The occupants of the van were thought to have stolen electrical equipment from a private house and were using the motorway to make a quick getaway.

It was what the police call a bandit vehicle. It is safer for the public if it is kept on the motorway and easier for the police to maintain their pursuit, allowing them to anticipate and forewarn drivers of potential dangers.

2. In this instance, the police decided to prevent the van from leaving the motorway at the junctions. It takes nerve and skill to do this successfully.

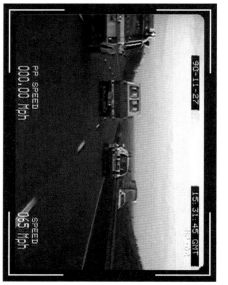

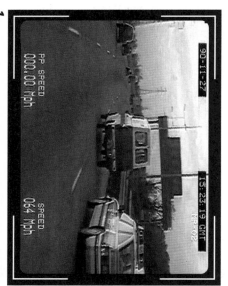

5.

6.

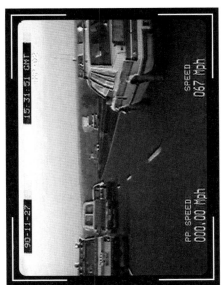

7.

8.

3. With another junction coming up, the police surrounded the van again and kept it on the M25.

4. The police were confident that the occupants of the vehicle were responsible for the burglary. But the video car had joined the chase after most of the electrical equipment had been thrown from the van, so it was essential for the video car to stay in contact to capture on camera any more stolen goods that they tried to get rid of, to use as evidence later.

5. Although it wasn't a TV or a VCR, as before, the video car did capture the passenger of the vehicle throwing out a TV remote control unit.

6. At the third junction the van escaped ...

7. ... but not for long.

8. Police radio: *He's crashed, he's crashed at junction 23.*

Fortunately, nobody was seriously hurt in the crash, but the driver did get an extra three months for dangerous driving on his two year sentence.

And Finally...

There are some events captured on video by traffic cameras which will never be repeated ...

Courting trouble

Bad driving can have unexpectedly cruel consequences. This driver (below) had been pulled over for speeding. But whatever trouble it landed him in with the police, it didn't work with his girlfriend, who was not amused. They argued for more than a quarter of an hour until the rather bemused officers decided they ought to be kind to the driver and book him. He tried to excuse himself on the grounds that he was only going fast because he was trying to scare her into shutting up. In spite of their spat, they got married soon after!

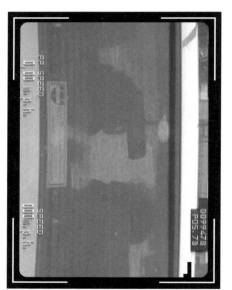

1.

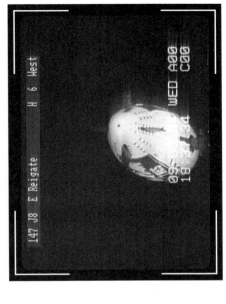

2.

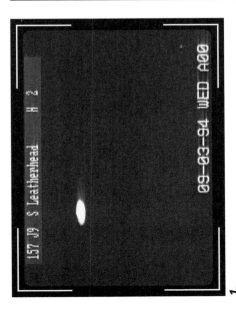

3.

The aliens have landed

Another event was out of this world, almost. One evening, police received a number of calls from the public reporting sightings of a UFO in Surrey.

1. The alien craft was recorded from a variety of angles on several different motorway cameras, and the Department of Transport observers could not believe their eyes. Was this the first time a close encounter with a flying saucer had been captured on video?

2. Drivers had become concerned when they saw beams of light coming from the craft apparently directed at the cars – were they trying to beam up a traffic jam to examine it? Evidently the visitors from another planet were without compass or maps.

3. But at last, with the help of another miracle of modern technology – the zoom lens – all was revealed. Sometimes even airship pilots get lost. And the pilot was simply trying to direct his spotlight on to road signs so that he could see where he was!

Death on the road

It was in 1896 that the world's first ever fatal road accident involving an automobile took place. Sadly it happened in Britain.

By 1966 almost 8000 people a year were dying on Britain's roads. However, although over the last thirty years the number of traffic fatalities has more than halved, the numbers of accidents and injuries is not being substantially reduced.

Now that there are over 25 million vehicles on the road, we are all going to have to take more care than ever before.

Acknowledgements

This book is based on the television series which, for the last three years Optomen Television has produced for Carlton Television and ITV. The production team must take much of the credit for the book as well as the programmes. Three exceptional directors, Patricia Llewellyn, Patrick Fleming, and Chris Kelly, have steered the series to success while, as researchers, Miranda Simmons, Grace Hodge, Kate Scholefield, and Nigel Paterson have trawled vast quantities of material to find the outstanding stories and clips. Lisa Beer and Susan Broom, the production managers, have kept the production firmly on course and, in front of camera, Alastair Stewart has been crucial in achieving a skilful and balanced approach to a sometimes difficult subject.

The advice and guidance we have received from Inspector David Rolands, Superintendent Paul McElroy and John Deal of the ACPO Secretariat, have been fundamental in building our relationships with the 52 police forces in the UK, and honing our awareness of road safety issues. Equally important is the perspicacity of Paul Corley at the ITV Network Centre, and Richard Simons at Carlton Television who recognised the potential of the series from the very first, and who have supported the programmes ever since. Anna Shelmerdine and Jo Miller have been organisational marvels in coordinating the additional material for the book. My editor Emma Callery was undeservedly patient and always precise, and Fiona MacIntyre at Ebury Press has once again demonstrated her unsurpassed understanding of the art of television publishing.

Picture acknowledgements

The illustrations in this book are reproduced with the kind permission of the following:

Central Motorway Police Group
Cheshire Constabulary
Derbyshire Constabulary
Dorset Police
Grampian Police
Hampshire Constabulary
Merseyside Police
Metropolitan Police Service
Norfolk Constabulary
Royal Ulster Constabulary
South Yorkshire Constabulary
Surrey Police
Thames Valley Police
West Mercia Constabulary
West Midland Police
Central Counties Air Operations Unit
Dyfed Powys Police Air Support Unit
Thames Valley Air Support Unit
South East Region Police Air Support Unit
Arkansas State Police
California Highway Patrol
City of Jackson, Missouri
Los Angeles County Sheriff's Department

Maine State Police
Minnesota Department of Public Safety
Mississippi Highway Patrol
Ontario Provincial Police
South Carolina Highway Patrol
Sudwestfunk
US Coastguard, Miami
Stockholm Trafic Polisen
Trafic Afdelingen, Denmark
Bob Tur LA News
Leo de Haas TV Produkties
Department of Transport
Automobile Association Archives
Accident Research Unit, University of Nottingham
Aeroplane Monthly
Agema Infrared Systems
Corporation of London
GATSO Cameras
JaiVision
McAlpine Helicopters
Transport Research Laboratory
Trevor and Vaughn Millard
Bryn Elliot
Metropolitan Police Traffic Museum